TAME YOUR BOSS

A Guide to Successful Living

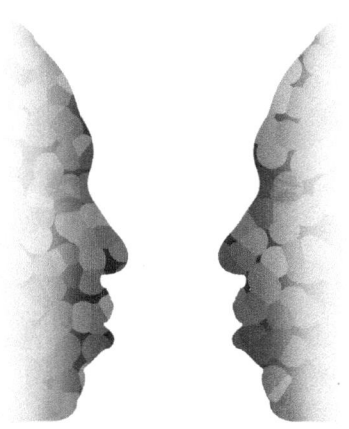

David Griffith-Sackey

9/1/19

TAME YOUR
BOSS

With best wishes !

DAVID GRIFFITH-SACKEY

David Griffith-Sackey

AMBASSADOR INTERNATIONAL
GREENVILLE, SOUTH CAROLINA & BELFAST, NORTHERN IRELAND

www.ambassador-international.com

TAME YOUR BOSS

Paperback: ISBN: 978-1-62020-893-9
eBook: ISBN: 978-1-62020-898-4

Printed in the UK

Bible quotations taken from KJV, NKJV, NIV, CEV, GW, NLT versions of the Bible.
Scripture taken from the NEW KING JAMES VERSION®
Copyright© 1982 by Thomas Nelson, Inc. Used by permission.
All rights reserved.
Scripture taken from NEW INTERNATIONAL VERSION ®
Copyright© 1973, 1978, 1984, 2011 by Biblica, Inc.™
Used by permission of Zondervan
Scripture taken from the CONTEMPORARY ENGLISH VERSION
copyright© 1995 by the American Bible Society. Used by permission
Scripture taken from GOD'S WORD®
copyright© 1995 by God's Word to the Nations. All rights reserved
Scriptures taken from the NEW LIVING TRANSLATION,
Copyright© 1996, 2004, 2007 by Tyndale House Foundation. Used by permission of Tyndale House Publishers, Inc., Carol Stream, Illinois 60188. All rights reserved. Used by permission

Ambassador International
Emerald House
411 University Ridge, Suite B14
Greenville, SC 29601
www.ambassador-international.com

Ambassador Books and Media
The Mount
2 Woodstock Link
Belfast, BT6 8DD, Northern Ireland, UK
www.ambassadormedia.co.uk

DEDICATION

To the author and finisher of my faith, Jesus Christ; thank you for my life and for trusting me with this book.

To my beloved wife of over twenty years, Donna; thank you for your love, unrelenting support, counsel and encouragement.

To my precious children, Charmaine and Jada, and my wonderful nephews and niece; this book is born out of your willingness to take my counsel on numerous occasions, and your showing me how important and necessary this message is in our world today. I love you all and I thank you for your love.

To my parents, David Snr and Margaret; thank you for raising me to become the man I am today, instilling in me the right values and creating the safe, amazing family we have and enjoy. I love you both dearly.

To my pastor, Adebayo Ademiju; it is without question that your teachings and guidance have contributed greatly to the person I am today – thank you.

Thoughtful and inspiring, this book offers a structured approach to finding yourself, defining your dreams and qualities you need to develop to get you there. You cannot but be impressed by the sheer depth of David's undertaking. His own spirit, passion and conviction shine through the pages, making it an engaging and enjoyable read.

Elena Shaftan, Psychotherapist.

David has a remarkable insight into the difficulties the less privileged in our society face in attaining their desired ambitions. His written guidance is a template in understanding the pitfalls we are all prone to fall into as we live our modern lives.

Anthony Nutt, Investor/Fund Management Director, Rtd.

There's an old African proverb that says; "What an elderly person can see lying down, a child cannot see it even if they climbed a tree". In this book, David has done a terrific job in climbing up the tree and coming down again to tell the next generation how to prepare for what lies ahead. It is particularly impressive how he has taken proven spiritual principles and translated them into a language we can all understand.

Adebayo Ademiju, Senior Pastor.

CONTENTS

CONTENTS

PREFACE

Dear Friend,

Do any of these statements strike a chord with you?

- I know exactly what I want to achieve in life; I just need guidance on how to make it happen.

- I have a good job and I'm doing okay financially, but I'm unhappy with my life.

- I'm capable of doing more; I just need to know how to unlock my true potential.

- Surely there must be more to life than this – I just can't figure out what to do with mine.

- Life feels too complicated, so I just follow the crowd with no sense of purpose or direction.

- I feel alone – if only I had access to someone who could give me the guidance I am looking for.

- I sure wish I knew how to 'make it' in life.

At one time or another, I have asked myself some of these same questions, and perhaps many more. I had a deep longing for something more, and I felt I was destined for more, but I didn't know what (or how to get there). However, after twenty-five years of searching for answers to the above statements, I believe I have now discovered a clear guide which serves as a solid road map for successful living. This guide shows how to take charge of our lives – to be the 'Boss' of ourselves and set the direction of our lives, to 'tame' ourselves so that we can cultivate the discipline to do the necessary things to achieve our goals – hence, *'Tame Your Boss'*.

As a young adult, I craved direction but didn't know where to turn. Like some of you, I was taught that a good education was essential to my success. However, life experiences and research taught me that whilst education is key, there was a missing ingredient to my success – LIFE SKILLS! Unlike the skills we are taught at school, university or at home, LIFE SKILLS (also referred to as soft skills or informal education) as a subject is not taught widely, if at all. LIFE SKILLS are essential to help everyone play the 'real' game of life and win!

My sincere hope is that, when you read this book, you will realise that you are not alone and can overcome any feelings of hopelessness, frustration, anger, fear or lack of fulfilment that you may be experiencing right now. I also hope that you are motivated to dream again – to pick up those dreams that you have dropped by the wayside and to connect with the greatness hidden inside of you.

In putting this book together, I have also been privileged to interview eighteen people who have had great success in their careers and finances, and thus to obtain invaluable nuggets on common traits, characteristics, mindsets and strategies adopted to achieve the level of financial success they enjoy today. I have shared their 'pearls of wisdom' in the career section of this book so that you may avoid some of the common (and painful) pitfalls that these great minds have experienced along their pathways to success.

Don't be mistaken; it will require discipline, time and effort on your part to learn, apply and live by the life skills and principles shared. But I have no doubt that this guide can work for you.

I am very excited for you as you start this journey and I wish you a renewed sense of purpose and a prosperous future!

David Griffith-Sackey

ACKNOWLEDGEMENTS

All accomplishments in this life involve the contribution and corporate support of several people in our lives.

I want to thank my wife and confidant, Donna, for co-writing and editing this book, and for making my thoughts pleasing in print.

An important aspect of this book is that it provides insights into the thoughts and experiences of eighteen people who have had great success in their careers and finances. The idea of interviewing these people was to obtain invaluable information on common traits, characteristics and mindsets, and the strategies they adopted to achieve the level of financial success they enjoy today.

For their generosity and kindness, I offer my sincere gratitude (in no specific order) to:

Algy Smith-Maxwell, Andrew Clark, Anthony Nutt, Ariel Bezalel, Edward Bonham Carter, Elena Shaftan, Gordon Davidson, Ian McVeigh, John Chatfeild-Roberts, Kevin Scott, Lars McBride, Maarten Slendebroek, Peter Lawery, Philip Johnson, Rory Powe, Sean Marriner, Stephen Pearson, and Tristan Hillgarth. Your contribution to this book is priceless – thank you.

ACKNOWLEDGEMENTS

Chapter 1

KNOW THYSELF

'When purpose is not known, abuse is inevitable'

This profound and powerful quote by the late Dr Myles Munroe really impacted my life. It challenged me, and sent me on a quest of soul-searching. Lots of questions started to flood my mind:

- Do I know my purpose – the real reason for my existence?

- Have I been abusing my life all this time?

- How do I find my purpose in life?

- Have all the choices and decisions I have made so far been in line with my purpose?

I can tell you that this soul-searching was not a pleasant experience. In fact, it was one of the most painful experiences of my life. Why? Because when I looked in the mirror of my life, I saw all the wrong choices I made, my stupid mistakes and the opportunities I'd squandered due to ignorance and misspent youth! Not a pretty sight! However, I persevered through this painful process as I ached for change in my life – I couldn't continue living with this 'void' in my soul. Once my soul-searching had ended, I came to the conclusion that, if I was to operate at my full potential and live a satisfied life, I needed to know more about myself and the reason for my existence. Who was I? What was I here to do?

Wouldn't it be great to have a manual that contained the answers to these questions! These were fundamental questions that

I needed answers to. And if you are still reading this book, you are also looking for the same answers.

Technology continues to advance every day; the latest mobile phones are soon replaced with another version with better features or functions. The question is, would you buy a brand-new mobile phone without the manufacturer's manual to refer to for instructions on how to access these new features? Not me! We can, however, figure out how to operate/assemble some things without referring to a handbook or manual.

I remember reading about an English man who bought a traditional Japanese coffee table (a Chabudai) and used it as a sitting stool at home. What he didn't realise was that traditional Japanese people sit on their living-room floor to have their meals or beverages, so the table must be of a convenient height. No doubt, there are many opportunities to abuse/misuse an item or a product if we are unaware of its usage or why it was made – which equates to its purpose.

From these scenarios, two key facts stand out: (1) *only the manufacturer of an item or product will know the real purpose for it and* (2) *to know the purpose of a thing, we must consult the manufacturer directly or the manufacturer's handbook.* Like mobile phones, TVs and cars, we (humans) also have a manufacturer and a handbook as a point of reference. This helps us to learn about our functions and the purpose for which we were created. So, who is our manufacturer? The answer to this question will vary greatly depending on your upbringing, culture, environment, values or beliefs.

I do not believe that you and I are here by accident – I believe it was by design. I believe that:

1. We were created (manufactured) to live and thrive in an environment called Earth

2. That our manufacturer is God

3. The handbook He has provided for us is the Bible

You will understand why these are my beliefs as I share with you the secrets I found when I discovered the Bible and the unimaginable, awesome power and ability that God has placed inside every human on the planet. I hope that you, too, will come to this realisation.

No man has been able to fully explain the mysteries of the universe. Neither do most of us completely understand the mysteries of the human being, gravity or electricity. This however, does not stop us from enjoying them. I believe that knowing God is my manufacturer gives me **perspective, purpose and direction**, otherwise my life is meaningless. We, like eagles, have the tendency to go it alone in life. However, when we encounter difficulties, we begin to seek help. Some seek help from God in prayer (as I do), some seek help in meditation and some may call on family or friends. Knowing God gives me comfort that I do not have to 'do life' alone, and I have the Bible as my handbook to guide me.

As promised, I will now share with you the awesome secrets that have totally transformed my life. The Bible tells us that we (humans) are created in the image and the likeness of God.

> *"Then God said, 'Let us make mankind in our image, in our likeness, so that they may rule over the fish in the sea and the birds in the sky, over the livestock and all the wild animals, and over all the creatures that move along the ground.' So God created mankind in His own image, in the image of God He created them; male and female He created them."*
> Genesis 1:26-27 (NIV)

No one has seen God, so how do we know what God looks like? The Bible tells us that God is a 'Spirit' (John 4:24). So, if I am made in God's image, then this must mean that I am also a 'spirit'. I also discovered that, just as God is made of three parts – God the Father, God the Son and God the Holy Spirit, referred to as the 'Holy Trinity' (Matthew 28:19, 1 John 5:7) – I am also made up of three parts: spirit, soul and body (1 Thessalonians 5:23).

To help me to understand my spirit, soul and body better, I discovered that my spirit is the realm of my 'sixth sense': intuition, gut instincts, faith. This is the 'real' me, the part of me that connects with God – **God-consciousness**. My soul is the link between my spirit and body, and is the realm of my mind, imagination, conscience, reasoning, emotions and 'will-power', the place where I process my thoughts and build pictures of things or situations (whether good or bad) – **Self-consciousness**. My body, the part we are most familiar with, is the 'suit' that contains my spirit and soul. Our bodies enable us to function in the physical realm in which we live with our five senses: sight, taste, smell, sound and touch – **World-consciousness**. This explains why we cannot survive on the moon without a 'space suit' to interact in its environment.

The diagram below provides an illustration of this phenomenon.

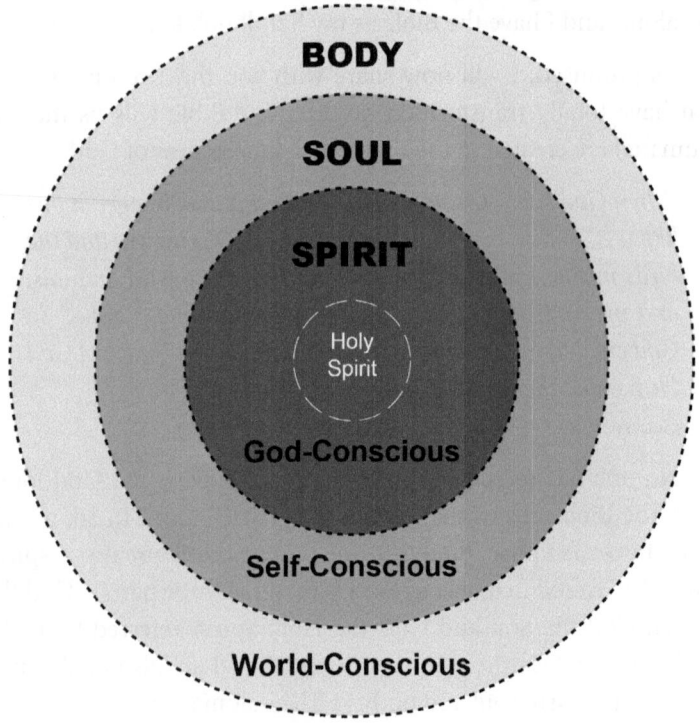

Once I understood and accepted this phenomenon, I became more and more fascinated with the 'spirit' part of my being. No, not like the ghosts in the films Casper or Ghostbusters, but the real me that I cannot see! Lots of scientific evidence exists about the body and the soul, but not a lot exists about the spirit. However, it is now scientifically accepted that we have a 'subconscious mind'. You may be familiar with other terms such as instinct, gut feeling, hunch, foresight, premonition, and discernment. These are words that describe the functioning existence of the subconscious mind.

Another word for the subconscious mind is 'submerged mind', which can be illustrated by an image of an iceberg. This image helped me to identify with my 'spirit-man' or 'hidden man': the real me that I cannot see.

You can see that approximately eighty to ninety percent of an iceberg is submerged in the sea, with approximately ten to twenty percent above the sea. So the ten to twenty percent of the exposed iceberg represents my mind and body, and the submerged eighty to ninety percent represents my spirit (subconscious mind) – a place of untapped potential! I came to understand that tapping into this potential was essential to designing my road map for successful living!

HOW WE WERE DESIGNED TO OPERATE

One of the greatest things that I discovered from the Bible is that whenever God wanted to create anything, He used His imagination to create a picture of the thing He desired, and then spoke out what He imagined. And when He spoke, it happened for real. Can you believe this! This was a game changer for me, because Jesus did what He saw God (His Father) do and got the same results; Jesus also got ordinary people (His Disciples) to do these things and they also got results. And if these Disciples could get the same results, that means I can get similar results, too, because I was manufactured in the image and likeness of God! This was not reserved for the gods in Superman or Hercules! Here's the source of my amazing discovery:

> *"In the beginning God created the heavens and the earth. Now the earth was formless and empty, darkness was over the surface of the deep, and the Spirit of God was hovering over the waters. **And God said,** 'Let there be light,' and there was light. **God saw that the light was good,** and he separated the light from the darkness."* Genesis 1:1-4 (NIV)

From this scripture, we can see that the creation of anything must first exist (in an intangible or invisible form) in our mind/ imagination before it becomes a reality or exists in a physical form. We can also see that when God spoke, He made a request (or command), and His request was carried out. By whom, you may ask? By the Holy Spirit – the third part of the 'Holy Trinity'.

> *...**the Spirit of God** was hovering over the waters. And God said, 'Let there be light,' **and there was light.**

God's request was carried out because what He had spoken precisely mirrored what already existed in His imagination. The Holy Spirit was God's key 'partner' – if God couldn't make this universe without Him, you and I cannot make anything happen in our lives without Him!

So, how do I know that God has an imagination and used it to create the universe? Well, when something is created, it is usually compared to a prototype or put in a frame of reference, to gauge how good it is. And since there is no record of God creating a prototype of a universe, but rather an original, it had to be His imagination that created it. This was His frame of reference – what God used to compare what was created and to confirm that it was good.

"God saw that the light was good, and he separated the light from the darkness." Genesis 1:4 (NIV)

How can you confirm that what you have created is good unless you have an original thought (imagination) or prototype to compare it with! Like God, we are to use our mind/imagination to create, design or construct a picture of the things we desire – in line with His plans and purpose for our lives, mind you! We then capture that mental picture by writing it down, 'speaking out' the picture of our desire with our mouths and waiting for the desire to become a reality! Like the law of gravity, this is a 'universal law' which is beautifully demonstrated in the Bible, in Genesis 1.

How do we create this picture? Through meditation. Meditation is simply constantly thinking about something over and over again, just as we do when we are worrying about something – we just can't get it out of our minds. Writing down God's plans and purpose for our lives also helps to crystallise our thoughts with greater clarity (thinking it through properly). So, when we combine the written word with the spoken word, it becomes a powerful, unstoppable force:

"Write the vision and make it plain on tablets, That he may run who reads it. For the vision is yet for an appointed time; But at the end it will speak, and it will not lie. Though it tarries, wait for it; Because it will surely come, It will not tarry." Habakkuk 2:2-3 (NKJV)

"Keep this Book of the Law always on your lips; meditate on it day and night, so that you may be careful to do everything written in it. Then you will be prosperous and successful." Joshua 1:8 (NIV)

The universal Biblical law only works on one condition – we must develop a deep, personal relationship with God through His Son Jesus Christ. This is to ensure that whenever we make our requests, they are in line with His purpose and plans for us, which are made a reality by the Holy Spirit!

"And I will do whatever you ask in My Name, so that the Father may be glorified in the Son. You may ask me for anything in My Name, and I will do it." John 14:13-14 (NIV)

This is how I believe we were designed to operate: to engage our desire with our imagination and to write and speak it into reality.

THE VALUE OF OUR IMAGINATION

Consider this; you are seven miles away from arriving at your best friend's birthday party and your car is about to run out of fuel! You need to find a fuel station quickly, and fortunately ahead of you you see two women in blue T-shirts and blue jeans waiting at a bus stop. You pull up beside them and ask for directions to the nearest fuel station. In following their directions, you continue straight ahead for seventy yards and make a left turn immediately after a pet-food shop with a red gated fence. After thirty yards, you take the second turning on the right and the petrol station is located on the left-hand side with a gigantic yellow signpost with red writing.

Now, did you create pictures in your mind to help keep track and make sense of the above scenario? Did you picture the two women standing at a bus stop, and did you picture or see an image of the red gated fence of the pet-food shop in your mind? What about the gigantic yellow sign post with red writing? I hope you did! It is well documented that we digest information by first converting it to pictures or images in our minds so that it will make more sense. Furthermore, before we describe anything with words, we have to have an image or pattern or design in our minds to match what we are saying.

Earlier on we spoke about the creative ability of God and how we possess the same ability because we are manufactured in His 'image' and 'likeness'. Please note here that the word 'image' comes from the word 'imagination' and this is why the imagination is such a powerful thing – it is critical to our existence and our ability to create the things we have in our lives, both good and bad.

Napoleon Hill, in his book 'Think and Grow Rich', writes, 'Whatever the mind can conceive and believe, it can achieve'. Can this be true? Absolutely! We see this truth in the Bible over and over again. You see, the imagination/mind is the womb of conception. A perfect illustration of this is the conception of a baby. Likewise, when an idea or thought (seed) is released or planted in our minds, the process of incubation begins, and after a period of care, nurturing and faith, that thought can become a reality. I discovered that, by developing the use of our imagination as God did, we can create for ourselves a life or a world that we never thought was possible. We can create a life (a whole life) beyond our wildest dreams.

The importance and relevance of our imagination can be summarised in this way:

1. Everything in life comes to us, from us (from our imagination or how we think).

2. We can't create what we can't imagine or see in our 'mind's eye'.

3. Every action we take is preceded by a thought (fuelling our imagination).

4. Every idea, thought or dream must go through an incubation period before it becomes a reality.

5. Over time, we become what we think about (the thoughts we create in our minds).

A great event in the Bible illustrates this point very well. Genesis chapter 11 tells us of a situation where a group of people decided to build a city and a tall tower that reached into the skies so they could become famous and prevent a situation where the group would be separated and scattered all over the earth. This alarmed God and He decided to do something about it:

> *"And the Lord said, Behold, the people is one, and they have all one language; and this they begin to do: and now nothing will be restrained from them, which they have **imagined** to do.*
>
> *Go to, let us go down, and there confound their language, that they may not understand one another's speech."*
> Genesis 11:6-7 (KJV)

Once again, the word 'imagination' is used here in the above scriptures as a formidable tool possessed by human beings for creating things, to the point that even God was concerned about the unity and drive of these people and had to stop them by creating confusion with different languages.

In the book *'As a Man Thinketh'*, James Allen states, '...Man is **Mind**..., and every man is where he is by the law of his being; the thoughts which he has built into his character have brought him there, and in the arrangement of his life there is no element of chance, but all is the result of a law which cannot err.'

What Allen is saying is that where we are in life is due to the sum total of our thoughts (conscious or unconscious) and not to chance. Quite frankly, the power of our thoughts (imagination) and our words cannot be underestimated. We live or die by the power of our thoughts and words! What a sobering truth! If we think and speak negatively, guess what results get? If we continually think that we will never amount to anything great, guess what results we get!

> *"The tongue has the power of life and death, and those who love it will eat its fruit."* Proverbs 18:21 (NIV)

Here's another secret I discovered about the importance of our imagination. **Purpose is useless without vision, and there can be no vision without imagination.** Equally, it is impossible to lead other people or ourselves effectively without vision. The late Dr Myles Munroe describes purpose and vision in this way: 'Purpose is when you know and understand what you were born to accomplish. Vision is when you see it in your mind and begin to picture the reality of it.' In other words, to fulfil our purpose in life, we must have a vision/goal/focus, and to create a vision we must use our imagination.

THIS THING CALLED DESIRE

'The starting point of all achievement is desire.' This is an undeniable statement of truth written by Napoleon Hill in his book '*Think and Grow Rich*'. He goes on to say: 'A burning desire, to be and to do, is the starting point from which the dreamer must take off. The greatest achievements of men, were at first, nothing but dreams of the minds of men who knew that dreams are the seedlings of all achievements.'

We discussed earlier how important vision is, and Hill shows us that the imagination alone is not sufficient for us to know and fulfil our purpose on this earth. We need another tool in our toolbox – a strong, burning desire. This desire is the fuel that ignites our ideas and thoughts, and sustains them before they are birthed into reality.

So, what is desire? It is a strong feeling of wanting to have something or wanting something to happen. Without question, we all need this thing called desire if we are to fulfil our purpose or achieve our dreams in life. Nothing of significance in the history of this world was ever achieved without it. Desire keeps us going even when the going gets tough and everything appears as though we will never achieve our goal or objective. How do we know that we have a burning desire for something? We can normally tell by the way in which we go after a thing. If we are hesitant and unsure when we go after a thing, then it is not a burning desire at all. However, when we really go for it with unrelenting drive, conviction, focus, enthusiasm and determination, and we make up our minds never to go back, then it is a burning desire. This kind of desire keeps us going even when we face obstacles and difficulties.

Now that we are aware of the need for desire, how can we stir ourselves up with so much passion and burning desire to go after a thing? The answer is to know our God-given purpose. Remember, purpose is when you know and understand what you were born to accomplish. Purpose is the number one stimulant to real desire. It stirs us up and produces energy to drive us forward with relentless determination until we achieve our goal. A life without purpose is a life without hope. And a life of hopelessness can lead to dissatisfaction, frustration, depression and stress, to name a few drawbacks.

Let me ask you a question: if you had all the money and resources you could ever dream of and also had the guarantee of success, what would you do? You may not have an answer right now, but one thing is clear: our purpose in life is aligned with improving the life of another person. Our number one objective is to discover our God-given purpose. Purpose is usually dynamic and changes from one objective to the next depending on which phase we are at in our life.

Knowing and going after God's purpose for our lives gives us a reason to live and to be excited about life. We get excited about getting up early and going to work every day. Purpose comes in all variety of ways: perhaps it is to help others, to make the world a better place, to innovate, to release people from poverty, to fight for the freedom of something, to change a particular circumstance or simply to raise your children. For example, one of the Bill Gates Foundation aims is 'to eradicate diseases such as polio, guinea worm, elephantiasis and blinding trachoma'. The overriding purpose of a charity named Centre Point in England is to end youth homelessness in Greater London.

One of the keys to opening the door to our God-given purpose is our unique gift(s) or talent(s). All of us have been blessed with unique gifts/talents/abilities, which may be hidden or obvious, but these gifts align with our purpose. They equip us to fulfil the purpose for which we are created. When we were born, these gifts came as part of the package, and it is our responsibility to unpack these gifts. You may not be aware of this, but other people are the beneficiaries of our purpose, and purpose is dynamic. Let's keep in mind that over time the focus or nature of our purpose can and will change.

To help you on your journey to discovering your gifts and purpose, take a few moments alone to think about the questions below:

1. What motivates me?

2. What am I good at?

3. What comes naturally and easily to me, even if I do not enjoy doing it for now?

4. What do people say I am good at?

5. What are the things I do that impact people the most?

6. What makes me so angry that, given the opportunity, I would like to change it?

If you do not already know your gifts and purpose, you must

work very hard and diligently to discover them. Knowing your purpose and gifts distinguishes you from the 'rat race' of life, and this is important. You can be fired from your job, but no one can fire you from your purpose because wherever you go, you carry your gifts and purpose with you! However, jobs (both professional and voluntary) and hobbies can help in identifying our gifts and/or purposes, so we should be eager to get involved in different kinds of activities, be they voluntary, social or professional. Doing this exposes us to situations which can help trigger hidden abilities or desires that we never realised existed. As a result, whatever we are given to do, we must do it diligently and seize every opportunity to develop our gifts and abilities.

When we discover our *God-given purpose*, we possess the fuel to ignite the flame of desire which in turn will help us to realise our true potential and fulfil our dreams.

Chapter 2

THE THEATRE OF LIFE

Now that we understand who we are and how we are designed to function, we are ready to go work on our lives.

The Irish poet William Butler Yeats wrote, '*In dreams begins responsibility*'. This is a powerful statement, because we have a responsibility to shape our future – to be the 'Boss' of our future. How do we shape our future? In life, we will make many journeys, and every journey must have a destination and a timeline, otherwise we won't know when we have arrived! Without a destination or timeline, we cannot choose the method of transport we need. Likewise, our future is a destination with many stops or 'mini-destinations' in our journey of life. We must have a picture of what this destination looks like so that we can identify it when we get there. This picture of our destination is what we frequently refer to as our hopes and dreams, which are formed with our imagination.

As individuals, we are responsible for our own journey and must take ownership for the roads we travel (with God's guidance) to arrive at our destination (our hopes and dreams). Many years ago, I had great difficulty focussing on what I wanted to achieve in life and how to get there. As I meditated on this in prayer, the spirit of God impressed upon me to treat my life like a project and gave me ten specific areas to focus on. This instruction gave me clarity of thought and direction and much comfort. This has truly been life-transforming for me, and I am privileged to be able to share my experience with you. I remember reading somewhere that whilst it's good to learn from your own experiences, it's even better to learn from the experiences of others – so you can bypass some mistakes and get quicker results!

So, let's begin by understanding what a *'project'* is. The Cambridge Dictionary defines a project as *'a piece of planned work or an activity that is finished over a period of time and intended to achieve a particular purpose'*. Typically, all projects have a goal or purpose (what they are trying to achieve) and are broken down into smaller, manageable chunks (tasks) so that the project manager can have good control. The project manager produces a plan of activities including timelines for completing each task (a project plan). To monitor progress, the project manager sets key targets (milestones or mini-destinations) to identify when these tasks have been completed – which shows whether the project is on track to meet its goal and be finished on time.

If we apply this model to ourselves, we become the 'project manager', the 'project' is our life and the 'tasks' are the ten areas of our life that we will focus on, building a plan of activities for completing each task. For each task/area we must have a purpose or definite goal that we want to achieve, and a plan of how we are going to do it. Together, we are going to design and construct our lives with our God-given 'partner' and the tools He has given to us – the Holy Spirit, our God-given purpose, imagination and desire. As children of God, we are going to use our understanding of being creators from the previous chapter to frame our thoughts in our imagination before they become a reality.

Welcome to the 'Theatre of Life', the imaginary stage where we design, shape and play out our lives in our minds (imagination) before they become a reality! On this imaginary stage, we create a world where we can be anything we want to be and have anything we want to have in alignment with our purpose and gifts. This is the secret to obtaining what we desire in life: health, friendships, well-being, wealth and happiness. This is where we say, yes, I can achieve all things in life in alignment with God's plan for my life.

Yes, I can create my world in the theatre of my imagination and then, with care and nurturing, it can become a reality.

I mentioned earlier that 'everything in life comes to us, from us'! Why? Because we are creators just as God is. In other words, everything we currently have is what we have created – consciously or unconsciously. If we are therefore unhappy with what we have created so far, we are going to have to change the way we think. Remember, over time, we become what we think about (as a man thinks, so is he)! The theatre of our life which we create will not only transform the way we think but will transform our lives.

To demonstrate how this works, we need to select an object of our desire – let's use a Mercedes car as an example. It is important that we do not think about the means or the money to obtain this. We do not concern ourselves with how it's going to happen in reality – it doesn't matter at this stage. Next, we are going to define in detail the type of Mercedes we desire: model, engine size, colour and interior. This process is important, otherwise we could end up with any old Mercedes or a totally different car altogether. We are going to write down what we see in our imagination. This image is the 'seed' we are going to plant in the 'womb' of our imagination. When we write it down, we begin to see a clearer picture in our mind's eye. This is part of the incubation process.

> "**Write the vision** and make it plain on tablets, That he may run who reads it. For the vision is yet for an appointed time; But at the end **it will speak**, and it will not lie. Though it tarries, wait for it; Because it will surely come, It will not tarry." Habakkuk 2:2-3 (NKJV)

So get a piece of paper/laptop/notepad and start writing! We will use positive language in the 'present tense', as though it has already happened. This process may feel like goal-setting which is fine because in a way, the process embraces some of the techniques of goal-setting. Let's begin by describing the make, model, engine size, colour, interior specifications such as leather or fabric upholstery, interior colour, etc. Define the car in detail, to include the type of tyres and wheels. Regarding the interior, define whether it has heated seats, a music centre, satellite navigation, a sunroof, parking sensors, an anti-theft tracker, etc. Describe the vehicle right down to the last detail! Note – this may take some time, and may need a number of revisions, but that's fine.

When we are satisfied that we have everything down on paper, we are ready for the next step. Let's go over what we have written down but this time in 'dream mode', where, in our mind's eye, we visualise and see ourselves playing a role in this imaginary movie; this is the process of meditation. Let's see ourselves owning and driving this vehicle. Let's see ourselves sharing this joy with our families and friends. Let's try as far as possible to engage all our senses to make this 'imaginary play' as real as possible. Let's smell the smells, and feel the feels. It's important that this visualisation exercise is done as a colourful moving image (like a movie) and not in a static way like a picture, otherwise the reality of this will not sink into our subconscious mind. This process of meditation can take some time to master or crystallise – days or even weeks! Remember, there is no rush.

The final step in the process is to 'plant' this seed – the object of our desire. This is where we accept and believe that we have the object of our desire, and we speak out loud what we have written until every time we speak, we see the image we have created; our words and image have become one.

> *"Therefore, I say to you, what things so ever you desire, when ye pray, believe that ye receive them, and ye shall have them."*
> Mark 11:24 (NKJV)

> *"And since we have the same spirit of faith, according to what is written, 'I believed and therefore I spoke', we also believe and therefore speak."* 2 Corinthians 4:13 (NKJV)

At this point, we are ready to file the paper or document away. You will understand why this is necessary. This is not a case of 'out of sight, out of mind' because the object is in our mind – our subconscious mind/spirit man! The written words also continue to speak for us, as it says in Habakkuk 2:2-3. This is a very important step of the process, as if we truly believe that our desire will come to pass as per Mark 11:24, we will enter a phase of giving thanks to God and trusting that the desire of our heart will come to us! Additionally, because we have planted these words into our spirit or 'heart', we can't help but to speak them as *your words show what is in your hearts'* (Matthew 12:34 CEV).

Once our image and words have been planted in our subconscious mind, they are now in the hands of the Holy Spirit. In the previous chapter, we spoke about how when God spoke, the Holy Spirit performed the action, and it is the same here. This is why we file the paper away and don't look at it again until harvest time! A farmer doesn't plant a seed and then dig it up a few weeks later to see if it is growing; this would either disrupt the growth of the seed or at worst kill it! Instead, the farmer trusts that with watering, fertilisation and the right conditions the seed will germinate.

As we continue with our daily activities as usual, one day whilst out and about we will begin to see this Mercedes pop up on the road, in a magazine or an advert! This is an indication of our desire coming to us. At this point we do not think about the 'how' or 'when' or 'where'. All we say is, THANK YOU, LORD! Because we know now it is on its way. When this happens, we behave and conduct ourselves as if it HAS already happened – that we have received our new Mercedes! This is our faith in action! Ask yourself, how would you behave if having that new Mercedes was a reality RIGHT NOW? Excited? Overjoyed? Well, start behaving like that now, believing that this is guaranteed!

We can plant many seeds for any desire we want in our life. We can plant seeds for tangible objects or intangible objects. We can plant seeds for anything in this world that we want to be by using this simple process – be it spouses, relationships, jobs, businesses, careers, suppliers, children, etc. This is the way we were created to live – we are creators like the creator Himself, God, our manufacturer. Everything is possible in the Theatre of Life. We are only limited by our imagination, so make your dreams big and set your goals very high. Remember, 'nothing is impossible to him who believes'. If your imagination cannot stretch far enough, refer to books, pictures, or videos, or create a scrap book to help you get started.

So what is it that you want in life? Define it. Write down in great detail the object of your desire that is in your mind. Describe it in the 'present tense' so clearly so that you can completely see it. When you have finished writing it down, go over it again in dream mode (meditate on it), speak it out, and then thank God for it to confirm your acceptance, and then plant that seed by putting it away and it will start to materialise. Our faith or belief is the watering and nurturing required to cause our seeds to grow and become a reality.

> *"Now to Him who is able to do immeasurably more than all we ask or imagine, according to His power that is at work within us..."* Ephesians 3:20 (NKJV)

THE 'WHOLELIFE-10' PRINCIPLE

There are several areas of our lives that need our attention in order for us to feel complete, happy and fulfilled. For example, if we aim for financial wealth but don't have good relationships with partners, family or friends we are not likely to feel completely happy and fulfilled, or to enjoy our wealth – as we need people to share our lives with. Here are the ten areas that God showed me to focus on as a project to make my life 'whole':

1. Character: what kind of person do I want to be; how do I want to interact with the world and how do I want the world to see me.

2. Ministry or Vocation: my purpose or calling in life.

3. Spiritual Life: acknowledgement and relationship with God.

4. Family and Welfare: my relationships and well-being.

5. Health and Fitness: how I plan to maintain my health.

6. Finance: money, earnings and investments, not only for me but to help others.

7. Career: my contribution to industry and society – the kind of work I want to do.

8. Friends: the kind of friends I want to surround myself with.

9. Hobbies and Interests: extracurricular activities to expand my mind and horizon.

10. Education: this is about life-long learning and not restricted to formal education only. This continually enriches our lives and empowers us to continually make relevant contributions.

Collectively, I refer to these areas of my life as 'Wholelife-10', where each area is brought to life in the Theatre of Life and meditated on separately. Each area is grouped into a diagram which I have called the 'Wholelife-10' Wheel of Life.

The 'Wholelife-10' Wheel of Life

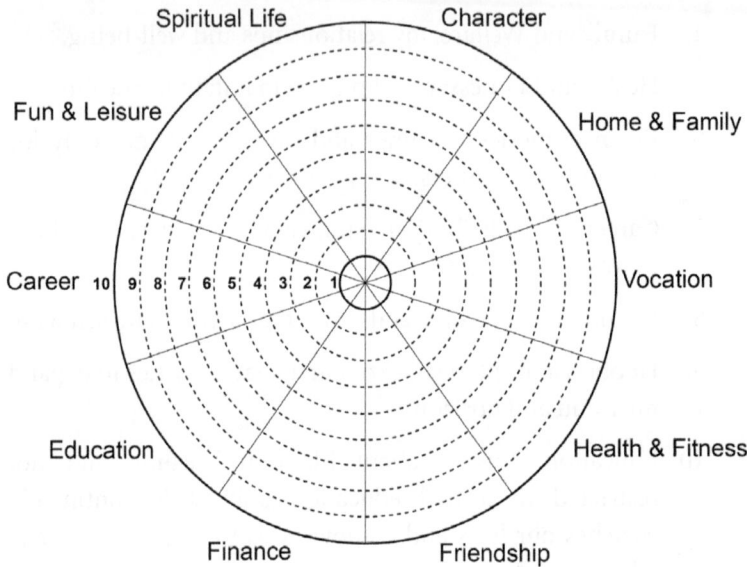

The 'Wholelife-10' Wheel of Life helps us to identify where we are currently in each of the ten areas of our lives. To see how well you are doing in an area, you rate your satisfaction level by placing a mark on the wheel. Point 10 represents very satisfied and Point 0 represents very dissatisfied.

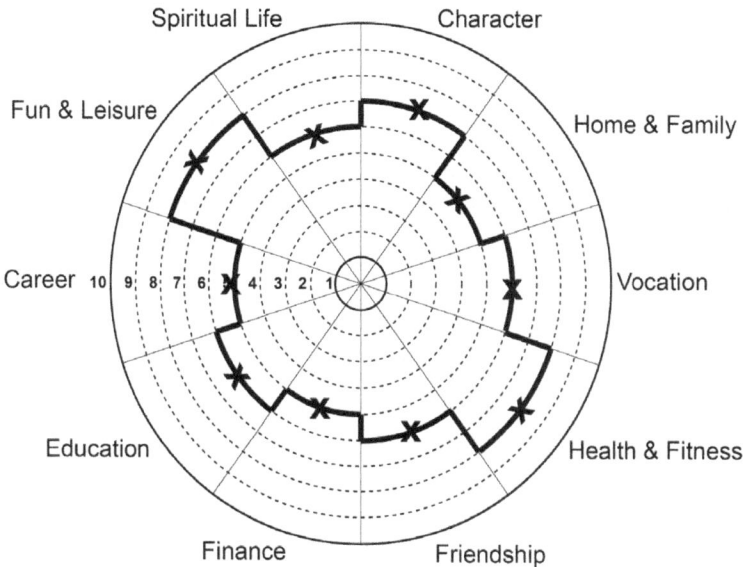

Now, depending on where you score yourself, begin to devise a plan about how to increase your score in that area. In the above example, this person might want to start working on Home & Family, Finance, Career and Friendship.

Once you plot your chart you can start work by:

1. Recognising the importance of this area and the difference it will make in your life.

2. Researching, learning or reading more about it.

Finally, bring that area into the Theatre of Life by:

1. Defining your desire for this area of your life.

2. Writing it down in detail, in positive language as though it has already happened.

3. Meditating (visualising) on what you have written.

4. Speaking out what you have written with confidence, as though it has already happened.

5. Thanking God for providing your heart's desire.

6. Go to work: apply what you have learnt from this book and from other resources – practise, practise, practise!

It is important to also include how you would like to see yourself behaving once this area of your life has been fulfilled. What would your life look like? What would your relationships look like? How would this impact your world professionally and socially? Write these down and use the above techniques to visualise and sow your seed.

Using the Wholelife-10 Wheel in the Theatre of Life has transformed my life and the lives of my family. I also believe that adopting and following these principles will transform your life and the lives of others: family, children, friends and colleagues. At the very least, it will help you to create a focus and direction, and in return you will have an abundance of hope, confidence and fulfilment. I am confident that you will:

• Discover and pursue a purpose for your life.

• Discover your God-given gifts and talents to help you fulfil your purpose.

• Shape and design your life.

• Achieve whatever you want.

As mentioned before, it requires discipline, time and effort on your part to apply and live by the life skills and principles shared, and I pray that these principles will help you to realise your infinite potential so that you can say to yourself and to the world, YES, I CAN!

"I can do all things through Christ which strengtheneth me."
(Philippians 4:13)

Chapter 3

The Person Specification

WHAT IS CHARACTER?

The strength of a country's currency determines the level of profitable transactions it can make.

Our name is the 'life-currency' we trade with when dealing with people in every walk of life, be it business, social, community or family life. Our name represents us just as a logo represents a company, and the strength of our name/logo is based on our reputation. How strong is your name/character (life-currency)?

Reputation is what others think we are; it is what people see in us and what they say about us when our backs are turned. Our character is what builds our reputation. Character is the person we truly are – what defines us as a person. Our character is made up of our attitudes, values, beliefs, perceptions and mindsets. These characteristics determine how we behave and do things, and **our behaviour creates our reputation.**

The Cambridge Dictionary defines character as 'the particular combination of qualities in a person or place that makes them different from others'. Also, the word 'character' is derived from the Greek kharassō (χαράσσω), which means 'I engrave'. As such, character is something that is 'etched into' us by the experiences that we have (and our response to these experiences) as we go through life. True character is shown in how we act or behave in any situation, and actions do speak louder than words in many circumstances.

It is critical to understand the importance of our character and how it reflects on the value of our name – the value of our 'life-currency'. Success in life is heavily influenced by the quality of relationships we build, and our reputation can make or break relationships either professionally or socially. Our reputation can either open doors of opportunity, or close them. Character is so important to our existence and the Bible encourages us to make every effort to build good character and to avoid situations that would affect us negatively.

> *"Do not be misled: 'Bad company corrupts good character.'"*
> 1 Corinthians 15:33 (NIV)

> *"But you, O man of God, flee these things and pursue righteousness, godliness, faith, love, patience, gentleness."*
> 1 Timothy 6:11 (NKJV)

So, what does your name represent? What is the value of your 'life-currency'? If a stranger mentioned your name to someone who knows you in a professional or social capacity, what would they say about you? What character reference would they give you?

TRAITS OF GOOD CHARACTER

I mentioned earlier that who we are (character) determines what we do, and how we do what we do (behaviour). The Bible is also very clear about this and it describes it slightly differently. It says that who we are inside (our spirit) determines the fruit we produce (behaviour):

> *"But the **fruit** of the **Spirit** is love, joy, peace, longsuffering, kindness, goodness, faithfulness, gentleness, self-control."*
> Galatians 5:22-23 (NKJV)

Let's look at some of the fruits we produce when we have a good character:

1. Integrity - Integrity is having strong moral principles and core values that govern your life. When you have integrity, you stick to living by these principles and values whether people are watching you or not.

2. Honesty - Honesty is not only telling the truth. It is 'walking the talk' – living the truth in all of your interactions, relationships and thoughts.

3. Loyalty - Loyalty is faithfulness – being devoted to your family, friends, colleagues and anyone or any cause with whom you have a trusted relationship/connection.

4. Respectful - This means treating yourself and others with courtesy, kindness, appreciation and dignity. It means valuing all people regardless of colour, race, age, how they look or how much money they have, and regardless of the position they occupy professionally or socially.

5. Responsibility - This is to firstly accept ownership for your personal growth and development, and for your contribution to society, either socially or professionally; to accept ownership and follow through on commitments to family, friends, work and church, and to accept responsibility for your behaviour and the choices you make.

6. Humility - To have a confident yet humble opinion of your self-importance. This is when you don't see yourself as better than other people or situations. To understand and accept that everything that you are and have is a result of God's grace, not your own effort or intelligence.

7. Compassion - To feel deep sympathy and pity for the suffering and misfortune of others, and to have a desire to do something to help or take away the situation that is causing their suffering.

8. Fairness - Using wisdom, compassion, and integrity, you make every effort to make decisions and take actions that will benefit everyone involved. It is about striking a balance to achieve a win-win situation for everyone.

9. Forgiveness - To let go of hurt and anger toward someone for an offence, whether or not the person is aware of the offence they have committed or whether the person chooses to apologise or not.

10. Authenticity - Being comfortable in your own skin – You are true to yourself and don't pretend to be someone else in any situation. Telling the truth always helps to make us authentic.

11. Courageous - Regardless of fear of failure, danger, discomfort, or pain, you have the strength to carry on with a decision or action, knowing it is the best thing to do.

12. Generosity - You are willing to offer your resources, time, energy, emotions, or positive words without expecting anything in return.

13. Perseverance - The persistence and determination to carry on with a course of action even when the journey gets difficult or uncomfortable.

14. Polite - Applying good manners to every person you meet.

15. Kindness - Expressing goodwill or good feelings towards others. You develop an attitude of helping others for their benefit and not yours.

16. Loving - To show through your words and actions how deeply you care about others.

17. Optimism - To demonstrate confidence about the future. You give a positive interpretation to life events, people and situations.

18. Reliable - You can be depended upon to deliver on your commitments and decisions. You do what you say you will do. You talk the talk and walk the walk.

19. Conscientious - You desire to do things well and to the best of your ability. You are diligent, careful, efficient, organised and vigilant in all your efforts.

20. Self-discipline - You have a strong sense of self-control to reach a desired goal. You have the willpower to overcome distractions (both good and bad) or feelings to stay focussed on a cause of action or commitment.

Character-building experiences take us out of our comfort zones and force us to 'dig deep' to find new resources within ourselves. However, we can begin by identifying the character traits we want to develop. The twenty traits listed above is a good place to start with.

The Bible tells us that we can only make a significant change in direction by renewing our mind.

> *"Don't become like the people of this world. Instead, change the way you think. Then you will always be able to determine what God really wants – what is good, pleasing, and perfect."*
> Romans 12:2 (GW)

Bringing Character to Life in the Theatre of Life

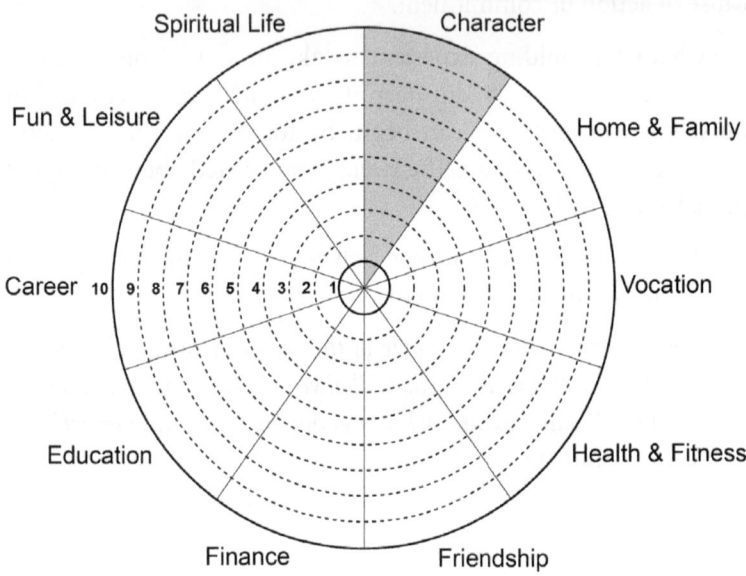

Know Thyself

The first place to begin on the journey to developing a good character is to identify where you currently are in the area of your character. Rate your satisfaction level by placing a mark on the wheel. Point 10 represents very satisfied and Point 0 represents very dissatisfied. You might choose to review the character traits listed above and identify the ones you wish to develop.

Make the Commitment

Depending on the score you gave yourself, begin to think about increasing your score in developing a good character by:

1. Recognising the importance of this area and the difference it will make in your life. How would you like to see yourself behaving once this area of your life has been satisfied? What would your life look like? What would your relationships look like? How would this impact your world professionally and socially?

2. You can choose to research, learn or read more about it. I recommend two books by Dale Carnegie: How to Win Friends and Influence People and How to Stop Worrying and Start Living.

Finally, bring that area into the Theatre of Life by:

1. Defining your desire for this area of your life.

2. Writing it down in detail, in positive language as though it has already happened.

3. Meditating (visualising) on what you have written.

4. Speaking out what you have written with confidence, as though it has already happened.

5. Thanking God for providing your heart's desire.

6. Go to work: apply what you have learnt from this book and from other resources – practise, practise, practise!

Chapter 4

HOME AND FAMILY

WHAT IS A FAMILY?

There are several definitions for the word 'family' and for the sake of this book we will focus on three definitions from Webster's Dictionary online:

1. The group comprising a husband and wife and their dependent children. This is the traditional definition for the immediate family.

2. The collective body of persons who live in one house, and under one head or manager. This definition can relate to a traditional family, or the wider family including uncles, cousins and house-help. This definition also relates to work, church, communities, school friends, etc: basically, a group of people brought together by a common cause. You will note from this translation that there is a leader for every group.

3. Those who descend from one common progenitor; a tribe, clan, or race. This definition will also relate to the wider ancestral family.

Depending on the environment and circumstances we grow up in, we will have a responsibility to one or more of these three groups.

THE ORIGIN OF FAMILY?

The origin of family is traced back to the Bible in Genesis 2:18 when God said, 'It is not good that man should be alone; I will make him a helper comparable to him'. He then formed Eve from a rib of Adam. Verses 21 to 24 say, 'This is now bone of my bones And flesh of my flesh; She shall be called Woman, Because she was taken out of Man. Therefore a man shall leave his father and mother and be joined to his wife, and they shall become one flesh'.

God established the basis for the family by bringing Adam and Eve together and established the principle that a man and woman would leave their parents and family unit to begin a new family unit by reproducing and multiplying in number. God also chose the structure of the family to help us understand authority. The structure of the family is vital to so many other laws, principles and teachings in the Bible. Once we understand God's plan for the family we can understand how relationships work at home, at work, in the community and in social circles. We begin to understand the hierarchy, structure and order that exist in these relationships.

BENEFITS OF FAMILY TO OUR WELL-BEING?

When we are born, we are helpless and depend totally on our family to provide for us, protect us, guide us and prepare us for the challenges we will face in the years ahead. It is at home that we learn to walk and to talk. It is at home that we learn or should learn to appreciate and share love for each other. It is through family life that we cultivate the habits, attitudes and values that shape our adult lives. It is through family life that we can be free to share our victories and freely express our disappointments. It is a place where we can be vulnerable without holding back. It is where we learn the social skills of loyalty, cooperation and trust. It is where we learn to love ourselves and each other, to bear one another's burdens, to find meaning in our life and feel the value of belonging to something more than just ourselves.

Everyone wants to belong to something. That's why we come together to socialise and have fun, support common causes, cheer for sports teams, and build villages, towns and cities. Depending on your circumstances, you may have had the great fortune of loving parents and siblings in a home where you could experiment and express yourself to build a strong identity, values and beliefs. If you had less than this ideal situation growing up, you still have the capacity to build families of your own making. You can create families through great friendships at school, communities, clubs, church or work, or even create a family environment with your spouse and children, whether biological or adopted.

The family is the essential, fundamental building block of society and every member has to work at building a successful family. Being part of a family is a big responsibility and there is a role for each family member to play.

HUSBAND

The principal role of a husband is to love his wife as he loves his own body. This is important because a woman needs to be loved and feel loved.

> *"Husbands, go all out in your love for your wives, exactly as Christ did for the church—a love marked by giving, not getting. Christ's love makes the church whole. His words evoke her beauty. Everything he does and says is designed to bring the best out of her, dressing her in dazzling white silk, radiant with holiness. And that is how husbands ought to love their wives. They're really doing themselves a favour—since they're already "one" in marriage."* Ephesians 5:25-28 (MSG)

WIFE

The nurturing nature of a woman is key in her role as a wife and mother. In her role as a wife, she supports and helps her husband. Likewise, the husband also supports and helps his wife, creating balance and harmony in the relationship. A husband can feel 10 feet tall no matter what he is going through as long as he knows his wife has 'got his back'.

> *"Out of respect for Christ, be courteously reverent to one another. Wives, understand and support your husbands in ways that show your support for Christ. The husband provides leadership to his wife the way Christ does to his church, not by domineering but by cherishing..."*
> Ephesians 5:21-22 (MSG)

FATHER

Fathers are to bring up their children in the teachings of the Lord and to not provoke them to anger or aggravate them until they become discouraged.

> *"Fathers, don't exasperate your children by coming down hard on them. Take them by the hand and lead them in the way of the Master."* Ephesians 6:4 (MSG)

MOTHER

Mothers are to love their husbands and children, manage their homes, and be role models.

> *"By looking at them [Older women], the younger women will know how to love their husbands and children, be virtuous and pure, keep a good house, be good wives."* Titus 2:4-5 (MSG)

CHILDREN

Children are to obey and honour their parents. Obeying our parents in a respectful way adds great value to the family and our parents. Obeying our parents also comes with a reward. The Bible teaches that those who honour their parents will live longer lives compared to those who are disobedient, hateful and disrespectful to their mother and father.

> *"Children, do what your parents tell you. This is only right. "Honour your father and mother" is the first commandment that has a promise attached to it, namely, "so you will live well and have a long life."* Ephesians 6:1-3 (MSG)

SIBLINGS

A family unit must behave with respect towards one another. In the church, community or work place we are to respect and honour others as we would our own brothers, sisters, parents and extended family.

> *"Never speak harshly to an older man, but appeal to him respectfully as you would to your own father. Talk to younger men as you would to your own brothers. Treat older women as you would your mother, and treat younger women with all purity as you would your own sisters. Take care of any widow who has no one else to care for her. But if she has children or grandchildren, their first responsibility is to show godliness at home and repay their parents by taking care of them. This is something that pleases God."*
> I Timothy 5:1-3 (NLT)

FAMILY, CHURCH, COMMUNITY, WORK AND SOCIETY IN GENERAL

Once we appreciate the family structure God has established, we can get a better understanding of how God wants us to interact with each other. Every group of people gathered together with a common cause is a type of family and must have a leader or manager to maintain order and collective peace. Without a leader there is absolute confusion – people can do what they want without having to answer to anyone. Using the church as an example, Jesus Christ is the head of the church and He is the authority. We, as individuals are members of the church and are siblings with Jesus and each other, as God is our Heavenly Father through our faith in Jesus Christ, His Son. Equally, at school or university, and in community activities or the workplace, there has to be a family-type structure to bring order and respect so that the group can function effectively and efficiently.

DO OUR ACTIONS DIRECTLY AFFECT OUR FAMILIES?

Have you ever witnessed or heard about a situation where the good name of the family was ruined by a single member of the family? This is a sad truth but it happens all the time. Your actions or behaviours can either make your family look good or bad. Actually, your reputation can reflect positively or negatively on your family or the group of people you are associated with. Depending on your moral values, if you wanted to date someone and then discovered that their sibling is a bank robber or paedophile, how would this affect your decision?

PUTTING INTO THE POT?

Belonging to a family means everyone must step up to help each other and contribute to making things work. While our first role in a family is as a dependent child, the part we play continues to grow in importance as we mature.

Perhaps I can use the analogy of a pot to describe the relationship in a family. Imagine a family where everyone eats from the same pot. However, someone must put food into the pot to ensure there is enough for everyone to eat. If everyone contributes a certain amount of food, there will always be enough for everyone and this demonstrates collective responsibility. However, if one person decides to take from the pot and never put anything back (e.g. receiving gifts but never giving any / not giving moral support in times of need but expecting it in return), there may come a time when this behaviour will arouse family conflict and this person could be restricted from the pot. You earn the right to eat from the pot when you contribute something to the pot. It is our duty to care for those in our family. Whether parent or child, sibling or spouse, every one of God's children has a role in taking care of one another. We are to encourage our loved ones in their trials, listening to their worries, cheering for them in their efforts and successes, and comforting them in their sorrows.

Many people take pride in their family names and their heritage. Others spend time putting out fires caused by past mistakes and seeking to create new roles. Regardless of what has happened in our past, all of us can make an effort to nurture and strengthen our family ties. We must make every effort to ensure we are contributing our share of responsibility in making our family a happier and healthier one. We can do this by having regular conversations and show our care and concern to make the family ties even stronger. We must strive to create better understanding between the members of the family.

Creating shared experiences are some of the simple steps we can take to strengthen the bond and improve the level of understanding and caring between the members of a family. Social activities such as eating together, taking holidays together, parties, sporting activities, educational activities, and games are some of the activities that help to build a strong family unit.

So what kind of relationships would you like to build? Perhaps your family unit is perfect, and if so, you may want to keep it that way. If your family unit is less than perfect, you can bring it into the Theatre of Life to create the ideal situation and have this as a vision to pursue.

Bringing Home and Family to Life in the Theatre of Life

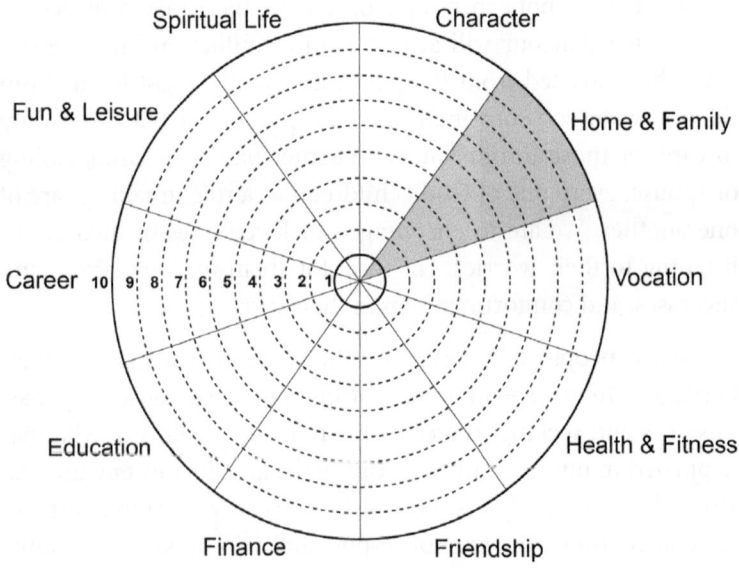

Know Thyself

The first place to begin on our journey to a great Home and Family life is to rate your satisfaction level by placing a mark on the wheel. Point 10 represents very satisfied and Point 0 represents very dissatisfied.

Now identify the kind of family would you like to have, regardless of your current set-up (Mum & children, Dad & children, or Dad, Mum & children; social family, church family or work family). Would you like a closer relationship with your parents, siblings, spouse, friends or colleagues? If there is an absent parent, would you like the relationship to improve with this parent? Is there a cousin, a friend or a colleague who just seems to bring out the 'dragon' in you, and you want to change that?

Make the Commitment

Depending on the score you gave yourself, begin to think about increasing your score to build a better Home and Family life by:

1. Recognising the importance of this area and the difference it will make in your life. How would you like to see yourself behaving once this area of your life has been satisfied? What would your life look like? What would your relationships look like? How would this impact your world professionally and socially?

2. You can choose to research, learn or read more about it. I recommend a book called God Guides by Mary Geegh. This book shows us that before we blame someone else for our hurt or pain, we need to look at our own contribution to the situation – whether it is five percent, fifty percent or a hundred percent, and take ownership and responsibility for that contribution, however small!

Finally, bring that area into the Theatre of Life by:

1. Defining your desire for this area of your life.

2. Writing it down in detail, in positive language as though it has already happened.

3. Meditating (visualising) on what you have written.

4. Speaking out what you have written with confidence, as though it has already happened.

5. Thanking God for providing your heart's desire.

6. Go to work: apply what you have learnt from this book and from other resources – practise, practise, practise!

Chapter 5

VOCATION

WHAT DO YOU WANT TO BE WHEN YOU GROW UP?

Did you come across this question as you were growing up – perhaps from a parent, friend, teacher, uncle or auntie? The answers we tend to give to this question at a young age are usually fluffy, but the situation gets more serious as we prepare for college and university. It is well documented that many people change their subjects or course direction once or more before completing college or university. After college or university, we enter the world of work, and even then we are not sure of the profession we want to pursue.

There are several important decisions we need to make as we get older, and deciding what we want to be is one of them. I believe this decision is more important than the decision to get married and have children because without knowing what we want to be, we are not in a position to build, maintain and sustain these relationships. When we start working, many of us begin to recognise what we don't want to do. Some of us may not want to be stuck at a desk or dealing with customer abuse, etc. At this point, we start looking for a job that uses our talents as well as giving us great satisfaction. This deep desire to seek a job that gives us great satisfaction and fulfilment points us in the direction of a VOCATION. A vocation is a strong desire to spend our lives doing a certain kind of work or activity – a sense of duty or calling that we feel gifted to do. So then, what's the difference between a job, a career and a vocation?

A job is something short-term, that we do for money. There is no long-lasting satisfaction or happiness from a job. Typically, we get into a job, outgrow it quickly and then search for the next job. We go in search of the next best thing that would give us that satisfaction or fulfilment. It is possible that we may be happy in the work place because of friends and the culture of the business, but even that is not enough to fulfil us. A career, however, is something with long-term goals that we pursue to make money. Many of us do not like our careers. A career may provide a stable means to get the money we need to maintain a particular lifestyle, while not necessarily bringing any fulfilment into our lives. We spend eight to twelve hours a day at work and are desperate for the weekend to come quickly so that we can have a break. The key difference between a career and a vocation is that, with a career, we separate our work from our personal lives.

A vocation is similar to a career but we also get deep satisfaction and fulfilment from our work. It is the kind of work that we will do even if we do not get paid. The work is so satisfying that it becomes part of our existence and our personal life. The rewards of salary and status are secondary, compared to experiencing our passion in a satisfying way. When working in a vocation we feel that our work contributes to a greater good beyond ourselves. We truly use our unique gifts and talents, and we feel that this is what we were born to do.

When it comes to life satisfaction and happiness, those with jobs are the least satisfied, followed by those with careers. However, those with vocations feel the most satisfied, because a vocation involves more than the work we are paid for – it involves the purpose for our whole life. When God created us, he designed us for a specific purpose. Each of us have a specific gift we were born with to make a specific contribution to the environment we live in, and to society at large.

"I knew you before I formed you in your mother's womb.
Before you were born I set you apart and appointed you as…"
Jeremiah 1:5 (NLT)

"The Lord has given them special skills as engravers,
designers, embroiderers in blue, purple, and scarlet thread
on fine linen cloth, and weavers. They excel as craftsmen and
as designers." Exodus 35:35 (NLT)

The gifts we were born with are what make us unique and different to anyone else on the planet. With our purpose and special talents, we are able to make unique contributions to the world and to others.

Another way to describe a vocation is a 'calling', because God created us with a unique 'call' or assignment. As such, we sense this call from within us to release these gifts so that we can make our unique contributions and experience complete fulfilment at the same time. Unfortunately, as we grow up, our true self is suppressed by the influence and expectations of family, friends, teachers and the media. Instead of listening to the call within us, we make decisions based on a need for approval, status and security. To welcome our calling, we have to shut off the voices of what others say we need to do and live true to our real self, with the guidance and understanding of loved ones if necessary. So, how do we discover our calling or vocation? Our calling is not one specific wonderful job out there, but rather our unique talents, gifts and capabilities combined with a purposeful passion or a compelling cause. It is very possible that some jobs may draw on different levels of our vocation. The ideal, though, is finding the kind of work that draws on seventy-five to a hundred percent of our gifts.

Our true vocation is a combination of our gifts/talents and our passion. Our passion is a purposeful cause that we contribute our gifts to achieve an objective, or to have a job that uses our talents in the service of something we are passionate about. For example, you may have a gift for investigating things, and a passion for a just society. As such, your true vocation might be becoming a policeman/woman, lawyer, judge or criminal investigator. Alternatively, you may have a gift for selling things and for negotiating, along with a passion for clothes. As such, your true vocation might be becoming a sales representative for a chain of fashion stores. You might be passionate about a cause, a country, a sport or a product. But you can also be passionate about a lifestyle or culture. If you have a gift for fixing things and working with your hands, you might be passionate about cars and engineering, and can find your vocation as a mechanic or a draughtsman.

Finding your vocation involves an understanding of what developed or undeveloped gifts lie within you so you can develop them to be the best you can be. As a child, you were probably aware of the things you liked doing and that came easily to you, and the things you didn't like doing and that didn't come easily. Unfortunately, we lose awareness of these gifts as we grow up due to influences from friends, family, teachers, television, magazines and the internet. The voices from these activities get louder and louder to the point where we are less sensitive to the voice calling inside us. We can improve our sensitivity to clearly hear the voice of God calling from within us. It is a matter of taking the time to carefully adjust the way we listen by taking time out for quiet moments of reflection through prayer and meditation. We must make time for activities that quieten and settle the mind: just to sit and think. To be successful at this, we need to be honest with ourselves and focus on what motivates us to do the things we do:

- As a child, what did you love to do? Write? Read? Do sports? Work on models? Play with a chemistry set? Spend time outdoors? Pretend to be a solider or a spy?

- During school group projects, what jobs did other students assign to you, or what jobs did you volunteer for?

- What do you enjoy doing the most?

- What do people say you are good at?

- What things come easily to you that others struggle with?

- What things do you do that impact and please other people?

- What things do you do for pleasure?

- If there was no restriction on money and ability, what would you like to do for work or for making change in this world or society?

- What aspects of your current job do you love and what aspects do you dislike?

- What kinds of projects and jobs at work and at home do you get excited about?

- What kinds of jobs do you dislike?

- When you talk to friends, which topics excite you the most?

- What things do you see other people doing that make you wish you were doing them?

- What issues get you so angry that you wish you could fix them?

- What dream has been burning inside you for as long as you can remember: the thing that always pops into your mind no matter how many times you dismiss it?

- What thoughts pop into your mind during the quiet moments when you are out walking, on the train or lying in bed?

- What do you think about always? Politics? Spirituality? Relationships?

- What were you doing the last time you totally lost track of time?

I suggest that you take some time to meditate on these questions, and the answers will come. Deep down we all know what our calling is. We all know what we really wish to do in life. What we must do is overcome any barriers, such as negative comments from teachers, parents or friends, and lack of money, resources, etc. The universal law of life causes resources to come our way once we discover and accept our vocation and then make a commitment to pursue it. So, in searching for our vocation, let us work hard to ignore any external noise, voices, distractions or obstacles.

Bringing Vocation to Life in the Theatre of Life

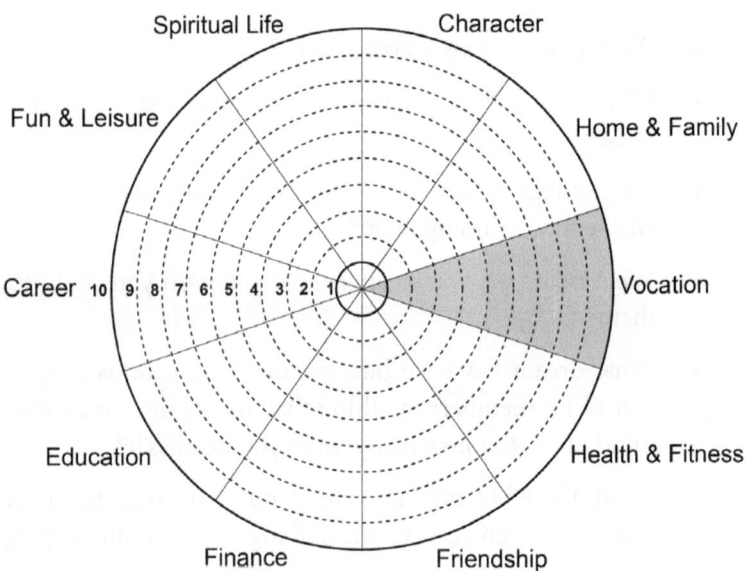

Know Thyself

Now we want to identify where we currently are in the area of vocation. Rate your satisfaction level by placing a mark on the wheel. Point 10 represents very satisfied and Point 0 represents very dissatisfied.

Make the Commitment

Depending on the score you gave yourself, begin to think about increasing your score to discover your vocation by:

1. Recognising the importance of this area and the difference it will make in your life. How would you like to see yourself behaving once this area of your life has been satisfied? What would your life look like? What would your relationships look like? How would this impact your world professionally and socially?

2. You can choose to research, learn or read more about it. I recommend a book called The Purpose Driven Life – What On Earth Am I Here For? by Rick Warren.

Finally, bring that area into the Theatre of Life by:

1. Defining your desire for this area of your life.

2. Writing it down in detail, in positive language as though it has already happened.

3. Meditating (visualising) on what you have written.

4. Speaking out what you have written with confidence, as though it has already happened.

5. Thanking God for providing your heart's desire.

6. Go to work: apply what you have learnt from this book and from other resources – practise, practise, practise!

Chapter 6

HEALTH AND FITNESS

"Dear friend, I hope all is well with you and that you are as healthy in body as you are strong in spirit." 3 John 1:2 (NLT)

Without good health (mental, emotional, physical and spiritual) living a productive and fulfilling life will be impossible. Our dreams, desires and ambitions will remain as thoughts only, without physical manifestation. Life without good health presents a challenge of monumental proportions and yet, as human beings, we are more prepared to plan for our financial retirement than to invest in our health. In fact, without good health we cannot enjoy our everyday existence let alone our financial retirement.

An interesting quote from the Dalai Lama puts it very well indeed. When asked what surprised him the most about humanity, he replied:

"Man.. Because he sacrifices his health in order to make money. Then he sacrifices money to recuperate his health. And then he is so anxious about the future that he does not enjoy the present; the result being that he does not live in the present or the future; he lives as if he is never going to die, and then dies having never really lived."

It is interesting to note that the journey of good health begins even before we are born. According to a research article on BBC online *(http://www.bbc.co.uk/science/0/22019289)*, while in the bellies of our mothers, our health can be affected by the lifestyle choices our mothers make. Studies have shown that if an expectant mother is highly stressed this may impact on her baby, leaving her offspring less able to handle stress later in life.

Heavy drinking during pregnancy can lead to foetal alcohol syndrome in babies, which can cause lifelong learning disabilities as well as physical problems. Smoking can also affect babies' development. Research also suggests a pregnant woman's diet can increase her child's risk of obesity by changing the unborn baby's DNA.

Being healthy is important because it can help a person develop a stronger heart and bones, better muscles, a sense of well-being and a better social life. Eating right and exercising regularly will lead to overall better health. A strong heart is the basis for our overall health and helps to keep the body functioning properly.

Normally we feel good in ourselves when we exercise and eat healthily. We are more energetic, alert, sharp, and focussed; we have more stamina to do things for longer periods and are generally happier in ourselves and better able to cope with the stresses of life.

KEEP YOUR MIND HEALTHY

Just as our bodies benefit from a variety of physical exercises, so do our minds benefit from various kinds of brain exercises. Equally, since our bodies get soft, weak and low in energy from a lack of physical activity, so do our brains. The brain gets lazy, sluggish and slow from too much routine or from lack of activities which stretch our thinking capabilities. Brain exercises are reported to help with the following:

- increased focus and concentration

- Increased mental stamina

- better ability to receive and retain information

- greater ability to understand complicated information

- less stress

- positive attitude

- increased flexibility

- motivation and increased productivity

- increased creativity

- increased innovation

- quicker thinking processes

- greater self-confidence

- feel-good factor

There are several activities we can do help exercise our brain muscle. To start with, let's look at some simple examples:

1. Physical exercise improves circulation and sends more oxygen to your oxygen-hungry brain.

2. Hobbies are a good method of keeping our brains engaged in fun ways; arts and craft, knitting, gardening, dancing, playing a musical instrument, singing, sports, travelling etc.

3. Regularly doing something new that we have never done before.

4. Spending time with different people from different backgrounds, to stretch our thinking through conversations and interaction.

5. Read, read, read! Read different books covering a variety of genres.

6. Try meditation; training your mind to be quiet can be really difficult. The benefits of meditation include stress

reduction, improved memory, improved learning ability and improved mood, increased focus and attention.

7. Puzzles and brain apps are also very useful if we find this stimulating.

8. Learn a new skill.

9. To avoid repetitions, take new routes or do things back to front, such as folding our hands differently, brushing our teeth with our less dominant hand or sitting in your less favourite chair.

10. Rely less on gadgets such as calculators, satnavs or spell checkers on computer.

KEEP PHYSICALLY HEALTHY

We can maintain healthy eating habits by avoiding unhealthy diets. There is tons of information on the web which I encourage you to explore so that you can be comfortable with the right diet which aligns with your lifestyle. Before we begin this journey of exploring good eating habits, it is important to have a basic understanding of a healthy diet. To get all the nutrition the human body needs, we must eat a balanced diet including dairy, grains, protein, fruits and vegetables, as well as fat.

As we all know, drinking more water is very helpful indeed, particularly purified water rather than tap water. Water increases energy and relieves fatigue. It promotes weight loss, flushes out toxins, improves skin complexion, maintains regularity of stools and boosts immune system. It's also a natural headache remedy and helps prevents cramps and sprains.

The body repairs itself when we are asleep, particularly at night, so it is important we sleep well every night. There is no health substitute for appropriate bodily rest. Adults should get seven to nine hours daily, whereas school-aged children should get ten to eleven hours.

Physical exercise or physical activity cannot be underestimated. It is quite simply the movement of the body that uses energy. Walking, gardening, briskly pushing a baby's pushchair, climbing the stairs, playing football, riding a bicycle or dancing at a party are all good examples of being active. Physical activity can be moderate, gentle, vigorous or high intensity:

1. One of the most common mental benefits of physical exercise is stress relief. Working up a sweat can help manage physical and mental stress.

2. Exercise releases endorphins, which create feelings of happiness and euphoria.

3. Physical fitness can help boost self-esteem and increase our positive self-image, regardless of weight, size, gender or age.

4. It improves overall brain performance, helping with decision-making, higher thinking and learning.

5. Exercising helps to keep us more relaxed.

6. Physical activity helps to extend your life expectancy.

7. One way to battle insomnia is physical exercise. It helps us sleep better.

8. It helps to strengthen our body muscles and bones, enabling us to do everyday stuff much better, such as walking, lifting, running, sitting, bending, squatting, pulling, climbing, pushing, jumping and anything else you can think of.

Bringing Health and Fitness to Life in the Theatre of Life

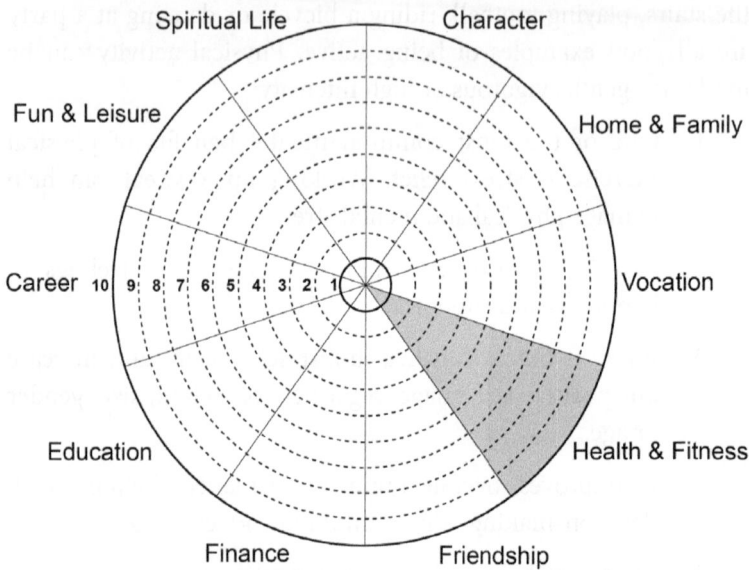

Know Thyself

Now we want to identify where we currently are in the area of Health and Fitness. Rate your satisfaction level by placing a mark on the wheel. Point 10 represents very satisfied and Point 0 represents very dissatisfied.

Make the Commitment

Depending on the score you gave yourself, begin to think about increasing your score to develop a better health and fitness life by:

1. Recognising the importance of this area and the difference it will make in your life. How would you like to see yourself behaving once this area of your life has been satisfied?

What would your life look like? What would your relationships look like? How would this impact your world professionally and socially?

2. You can choose to research, learn or read more about it. I recommend reading Dr Don Colbert's book, The Seven Pillars of Health: The Natural Way To Better Health For Life.

Finally, bring that area into the Theatre of Life by:

1. Defining your desire for this area of your life.

2. Writing it down in detail, in positive language as though it has already happened.

3. Meditating (visualising) on what you have written.

4. Speaking out what you have written with confidence, as though it has already happened.

5. Thanking God for providing your heart's desire.

6. Go to work: apply what you have learnt from this book and from other resources – practise, practise, practise!

Chapter 7

FRIENDSHIP

"Two are better off than one, because together they can work more effectively. If one of them falls down, the other can help him up. But if someone is alone and falls, it's just too bad, because there is no one to help him. If it is cold, two can sleep together and stay warm, but how can you keep warm by yourself. Two people can resist an attack that would defeat one person alone. A rope made of three cords is hard to break." Ecclesiastes 4:9-12 (GNT)

"Keep company with the wise and you will become wise. If you make friends with stupid people, you will be ruined." Proverbs 13:20 (GNT)

"Do not be fooled. 'Bad companions ruin good character.'" 1 Corinthians 15:33 (GNT)

Friendship is an affectionate relationship between people who have a stronger bond than that between associates. Many of us have people in our lives for whom we feel a strong affection or with whom we bond. They may be family members or persons from school, work, community or social groups.

Friends are drawn together by common interests, common backgrounds, common experiences, values and equality where there is a balance of 'give and take'. A true friend is consistently willing to put your happiness before any selfish agendas. A true friend will tell you the truth (even when it may be unpleasant) if it is in your best interest.

A true friend would not ask you to compromise your principles in the name of your friendship or anything else. A true friend inspires you to live up to your best potential, not to indulge in habits that would harm you eventually.

For some reason, a light bulb went off in my head when I turned nineteen years of age. I began to take my life more seriously; I focused more on my studies to gain a skill so that I could find gainful employment and began to distance myself from specific groups of friends who had a negative influence on the direction I had decided to take.

As I got older, and particularly now, at the age of fifty two, I recognise more and more the importance of people in our lives. I recognise that life is about people and relationships, yet maintaining relationships is the most difficult area of our lives to master. The scriptures above from the Bible describe the importance of friendship very well; however, there are severe consequences to surrounding ourselves with the wrong kind of friends and the Bible also makes this clear in the above scriptures.

So, it is about balance – every human being is important in God's eyes and this should be the case for us as well. We can strike a good balance by spending more of our time with the people who have a good influence over our lives and less of our time with those who have a negative influence.

What we don't want to do is risk a reputation where we give the impression that we are better than other people by only talking with or spending time with specific kinds of people. It is good practice to talk with everyone and to respect every person as an important life force on this planet because we never know when we may need to call on their assistance. A homeless person on the street can become a valuable source of information if they witnessed an incident in the area.

Solid, good friends play a massive role in our lives. The company we keep will contribute to shaping the person we become.

Having good friends provides us with a network of support despite the struggles and disagreements we may have along the way. Our bond with friends grow stronger with shared experiences from the good times and also from challenging times. Sometimes we can get frustrated with relationships and feel that we can't rely on anyone but ourselves. It takes time to build relationships based on trust, integrity and credibility, and even then, we sometimes experience severe disappointment from our friends because we have set unspoken expectations that they are unable to meet.

One thing is for certain; we can't control every situation concerning friends so, while working on these relationships, we should also use the time to focus on ourselves so that we can learn to enjoy our own company and love ourselves. We can't give what we don't have. We can't give love and enjoy the company of others fully if we don't learn to love ourselves first and enjoy our own company. So there are times in our lives when being alone is beneficial to our personal growth.

This said, we do not want to swing to the other extreme where we become loners. The reality is, no one wants to be alone, and being a loner may be a result of many things which eventually affects our confidence. It is essential that we cultivate a network of support with friends where we contribute by supporting others first, and by so doing earn their support when a need arises. For want of a better expression: we can't keep taking out of the pot and not putting anything back, because one day the pot will be empty. We can't keep expecting people to support us all the time and not provide support in return.

We learn more about ourselves when we spend time with friends. We learn about our interests, abilities, and gifts, how we deal with different personalities and situations, and our likes and dislikes. Friends help us to develop the critical social skills required to survive in society. Shared experiences create the best memories when we are a part of a group of special friends. Our life becomes far richer when we engage with people from all walks of life. We are on this planet to contribute our abilities and gifts, and every contribution we make should affect another person or group of persons, including our friends, family, colleagues or customers.

We also have a deep desire to share our experiences with other people. For example, if we buy a new car or get a promotion and have no one to share it with, we do not enjoy it as much. We enjoy ourselves far more when we are able to share these experiences with other people, particularly our special friends and family. When we are surrounded by good friends, we have a feeling of wellness, joy and happiness. Loneliness can affect our social and human relations skills which can cause us stress because we are not sure how to behave in certain situations and environment.

We were not created to be an 'island'. God created us to be inter-dependent; that's why we only have limited skills and abilities and have to rely on other people to bridge the gap. Therefore, human relations skills are critical in influencing and engaging other people, otherwise how can we live and work together effectively?

It must be noted that good relationships don't just happen out of the blue. We all have a responsibility to work at building strong relationships if we want to enjoy the benefits. Unless you have tried it, it is impossible to know the power of the fulfilment, enjoyment and motivation we get when we do things to enrich other people's lives, either through laughter, a compliment, a kind word, support, encouragement, fun, empowerment, development or simply making their lives easier or better through innovative ideas, etc.

Bringing Friendship to Life in the Theatre of Life

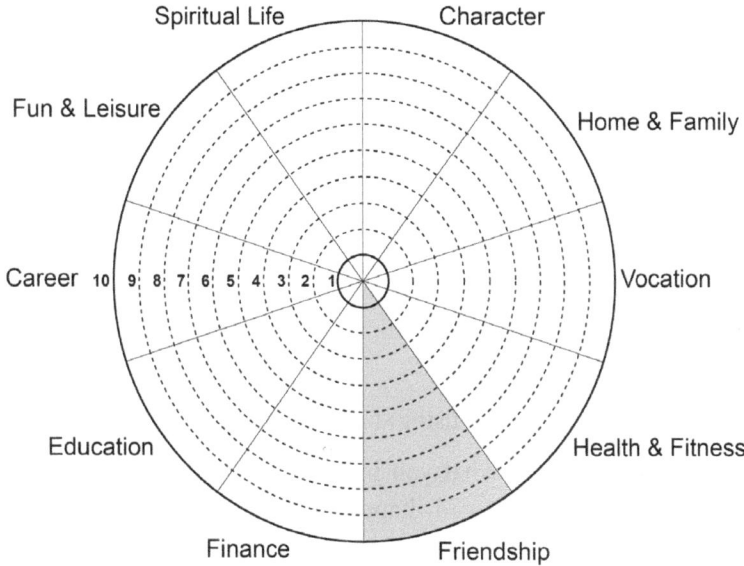

Know Thyself

First, we need to identify the types of friendships we currently have that we wish to change or develop. Rate your satisfaction level by placing a mark on the wheel. Point 10 represents very satisfied and Point 0 represents very dissatisfied.

Make the Commitment

Depending on the score you gave yourself, begin to think about increasing your score to build better friendships by:

1. Recognising the importance of this area and the difference it will make in your life. How would you like to see yourself behaving once this area of your life has been satisfied?

What would your life look like? What would your relationships look like? How would this impact your world professionally and socially?

2. You can choose to research, learn or read more about it. Again, I refer you to How to Win Friends and Influence People by Dale Carnegie (recommended in Chapter 3). This book shows practical ways to win with people.

Finally, bring that area into the Theatre of Life by:

1. Defining your desire for this area of your life.

2. Writing it down in detail, in positive language as though it has already happened.

3. Meditating (visualising) on what you have written.

4. Speaking out what you have written with confidence, as though it has already happened.

5. Thanking God for providing your heart's desire.

6. Go to work: apply what you have learnt from this book and from other resources – practise, practise, practise!

Chapter 8

FINANCE

Money is at the heart of every financial transaction and, as such, it is an important tool we use in modern life. Understanding how this tool works is key. A lack of understanding of this tool and how the monetary system works can result in frustration, stress, depression and substandard living, all of which can lead to debt, theft, fraud, depression and conflict.

In simple terms, money is a means of exchange. It is a way for a person to trade what he has for what he wants. To properly understand this concept, we must go back to the methods of trading before money was invented.

The previous way of trading was referred to as direct barter. For example, a farmer who produced rice but wanted clothes for his family would search for someone who had or made clothes but also had a need for rice. This method of trading involved finding that perfect person – so you can imagine the difficulty in doing this, particularly with no modern private and public transportation, internet, emails, social media or telephone.

The difficulty of this method led to indirect barter. So, for example, if the rice farmer found a clothes maker but learned that the clothes maker had no need for rice but had a need for carrots, the rice farmer would keep that in mind; if he discovered someone expressing a need for rice in exchange for carrots, he would trade his rice for carrots and then trade the carrots with the clothes maker.

Food became a necessary and highly exchangeable product for this method of trading, bringing about another issue of durability. Food is a perishable product, so people had to trade it before it rotted or went off. Thus, over a period of time non-perishable goods such as silver and gold became the ideal and preferred means of trading because they did not rot or rust.

Further, with this method of trading it was very difficult to gauge the precise exchange value of goods in units of sacks of rice, clothes or carrots. As such, the method of exchange progressed to the use of fixed weights of gold and silver as a means of exchange to the exact value of the goods. Much better progress was made using this method.

This method of weighted gold and silver then evolved to what we now know as paper money printed and distributed by the banks. This transition to banknotes began when miners would bring their gold to the goldsmiths for moulding. In return, the goldsmith would give the miner a receipt as proof of ownership that he could then use to claim his moulded coins when production was completed.

Rather than waiting for the production to be completed, the miner discovered that he could trade his receipt (his proof of ownership of the gold) for goods and return to the mines without having to wait for his gold. This level of transaction transferred ownership of the gold to the person who handed over the goods to the miner. Over time, this method of transaction became popular and these receipts became a means of exchange for goods and services.

This method of transaction was later adopted by the central banks to help facilitate a convenient means of exchange for access to goods and services. In essence, the banknote is like a promise note (an 'I owe you' note); we should be careful not to always think of money as a physical thing or something that has intrinsic value. Money only represents a certain value, but the money object itself (the banknote itself) does not necessarily have intrinsic value.

Although important, money should not be confused with true wealth. It is only a tool – a means of exchange. Although money is a necessary component of modern life, it is not a necessary component for acquiring true wealth. True wealth has different meanings to different people, and in most cases it involves other needs such as companionship, good friends, good family, good health, good career, access to shelter, access to food, access to water, security and more. Money makes it more convenient to achieve certain things in life, but money and true wealth should not always be thought of as the same thing.

I read somewhere that confusing money with true wealth is like confusing a meal ticket with the actual meal. Although we need the meal ticket to have the meal, the quality of the meal is not dependent on the ticket. While money can certainly make it easier to purchase material things, and can even bring about some level of happiness, it is always a means to an end and should not be confused with the end itself.

Since the banknote itself has no intrinsic value, we have to trade something (product or service) in order to receive money; this product or service is called 'work'. Without working we cannot expect money to come to us by osmosis. We have to trade something of value; in return we receive money. By value I mean our ability (physical/mental), talent, skill, knowledge, wisdom, etc. We trade value through work – job, career or vocation.

So now that we have the money, what do we do with it? If all we do is spend the money as soon as we receive it, there is a strong possibility that we will always live in poverty. A wiser approach would be to create additional wealth with the money we earn – building a surplus, so that we can live a comfortable and hopefully debt-free life.

It would be inaccurate for anyone to say they are truly rich and living an abundant life if they do not have a sustainable surplus which will stretch to being generous to charitable causes, the less fortunate, friends, family, etc.

"And God will generously provide all you need. Then you will always have everything you need and plenty left over to share with others" 2 Corinthians 9:8 (NLT)

So, as seen clearly in the scripture above, wealth accumulation is not only for our use. We should all have a greater purpose and focus apart from ourselves. It is a fact that we experience a much better existence when we are able to give to others. If you have never tried it before, then this is a good time to try to be a giver without expecting anything in return. It is an amazing feeling of well-being when we give or contribute to making a situation or someone's life better. Literally, our life experience is much, much richer and fulfilling when we are generous towards others.

There are many routes to acquiring financial wealth and for some people it can lead to destruction if money-making is the sole focus of their lives or is achieved by devious means.

"Wealth from get-rich-quick schemes quickly disappears; wealth from hard work grows over time." Proverbs 13: 11 (NLT)

There are credible ways to create sustainable financial wealth. However, they require working and applying oneself. All too often, laziness and a lack of patience result in get-rich-quick schemes, and this approach usually leads to destruction.

"Take a lesson from the ants, you lazybones. Learn from their ways and become wise! Though they have no prince or governor or ruler to make them work, they labour hard all summer, gathering food for the winter. But you, lazybones, how long will you sleep? When will you wake up? A little extra sleep, a little more slumber, a little folding of the hands to rest— then poverty will pounce on you like a bandit; scarcity will attack you like an armed robber."
Proverbs 6:11 (NLT)

Financial wealth accumulation requires work, wisdom, persistence and diligence, and I am truly encouraged to share with you some principles that will start you on your journey.

"But divide your investments among many places, for you do not know what risks might lie ahead." Ecclesiastes 11:2 (NLT)

So let's look at a few simple but powerful principles that can help us manage and increase our financial wealth.

Principle No. 1 – Work

To begin with, we must work hard at cultivating a skill, knowledge or talent and use this as a valuable product in transaction to earn money. We trade our ability (or give value) in exchange for money. We can do this by identifying what we are good at and then, through education, training and practice, developing this ability to the level where we can exchange this through work for money.

Principle No. 2 – Pay Yourself First

Once we start earning money we should endeavour to save at least ten percent of our total

income every week, month or however frequently we get paid. Regardless of how much we earn we should learn to live on the remaining ninety percent. Strangely enough, we get used to living on the remainder once we put it into practice.

Principle No. 3 – Spend Your Money

When spending our money, there are two things to consider: Essentials and Nice-to-haves. The essentials are necessary expenses such as rent, utility bills, food, clothing, etc. The nice-to-haves will mean different things to different people. For example, an extra television in my bedroom when we have one in the living room is a nice-to-have and not a necessity. Make a distinction between the Essentials and the Nice-to-haves and cultivate the habit of budgeting to help to control your spending.

Principle No. 4 – Increase Your Money

Saving is good and essential; however, if we want to create wealth we need to multiply the money we earn. Investing our money is a good way to multiply it and there are various ways of doing this, such as through stocks and shares, bonds, property and pensions, to name only a few. It is well worth looking into this and speaking with the right people for guidance. Delayed gratification and investing for our future is a sure way of enjoying greater benefits later in our lives.

Principle No. 5 – Continual Self-Development

While our hard-earned money is working hard for us through savings and investments, we must also find ways to develop ourselves to attract higher earnings. Our world is continually evolving and change is a constant; as such, we will have many opportunities to train in a new skill or to improve on what we do to make us more valuable and marketable, and to earn more.

The topic of finance and wealth creation is a vast one, and there are several books to choose from to expand your knowledge. I can help you start your journey of reading by recommending the following books which I am sure you will find extremely helpful:

'Rich Dad Poor Dad', written by Robert Kiyosaki and Sharon Lechter. This book advocates the importance of financial independence and building wealth through investing and real-estate investing, as well as increasing one's financial intelligence to improve one's business and financial aptitude.

'The Richest Man in Babylon', written by George Samuel Clason. This book provides financial advice through experiences in business and managing household finances by using characters and providing simple lessons in financial wisdom.

'*The Millionaire Next Door*', written by Thomas J. Stanley and William D. Danko. This book provides advice to help people achieve a higher net worth compared to their income.

Bringing Finance to Life in the Theatre of Life

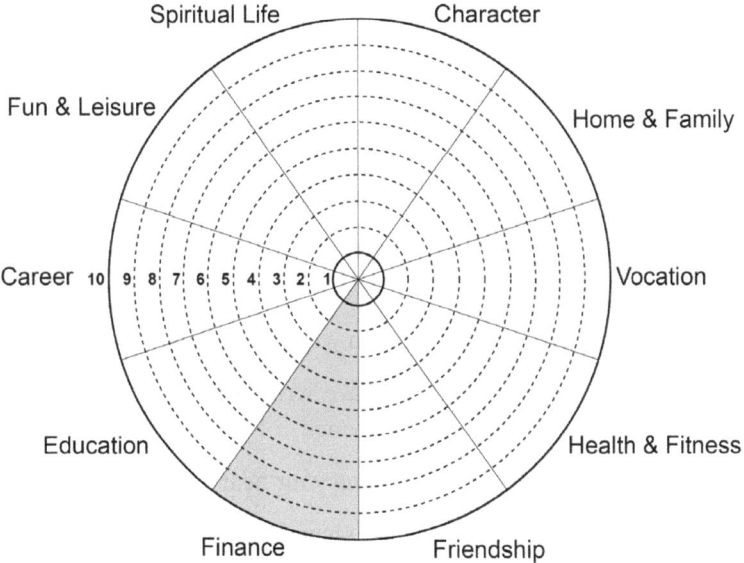

Know Thyself

Now we want to identify where we currently are in the area of Finance. Rate your satisfaction level by placing a mark on the wheel. Point 10 represents very satisfied and Point 0 represents very dissatisfied.

Make the Commitment

Depending on the score you gave yourself, begin to think about to increasing and sustaining a healthy financial wealth by:

1. Recognising the importance of this area and the difference it will make in your life. How would you like to see yourself behaving once this area of your life has been satisfied? What would your life look like? What would your relationships look like? How would this impact your world professionally and socially?

2. You can choose to research, learn or read more about it. I encourage you to read the books recommended above.

Finally, bring that area into the Theatre of Life by:

1. Defining your desire for this area of your life.

2. Writing it down in detail, in positive language as though it has already happened.

3. Meditating (visualising) on what you have written.

4. Speaking out what you have written with confidence, as though it has already happened.

5. Thanking God for providing your heart's desire.

6. Go to work: apply what you have learnt from this book and from other resources – practise, practise, practise!

Chapter 9

EDUCATION

> *"It is better – much better – to have wisdom and knowledge than gold and silver."* Proverbs 16:16 (GNT)
>
> *"Everyone who lives ought to be wise; it is as good as receiving an inheritance and will give you as much security as money can. Wisdom keeps you safe – this is the advantage of knowledge."* Ecclesiastes 7:11-12 (GNT)

At the most basic level, education is critically important because it gives people the foundational skills to survive in this world. Education equips people with the knowledge and confidence to contribute to their community and country. As well as providing people with knowledge, education helps to instil values and transforms attitudes and behaviours. Education is one of the best means for social change, economic development and prosperity of a country. Nelson Mandela once said, 'Education is the most powerful weapon which you can use to change the world'.

Education is a life-long process. It is not a case of reading a book and passing an examination, and then we are finished with education. From the day we are born until the day we die, our existence is a process of learning. Formal education teaches us how to take ownership of our lives, be responsible and manage ourselves. During our education, we will have several opportunities to make sacrifices to study for exams and write assignments. Once we take responsibility for this journey, we learn more about ourselves and our capability. We learn how to reason using logic as we write assignments and develop our abilities to put forward arguments to reinforce our opinions. We learn critical analytical skills which help us consider situations and make balanced decisions.

Another great aspect about education is that we are presented with several opportunities to interact with people with different personalities. When we are exposed to people from all walks of life we discover new points of view, learn to appreciate diversity and differences in opinions, grow as people and develop social skills. Embracing diversity also gives us a much better view of the world and helps to develop our understanding of important events that are occurring in it.

Most of our good friendships are created throughout our education, simply because we spend a large amount of our time with our peers either individually or through group activities or social functions. Spending this amount of time together helps us to know others better and share common interest and experiences with them; in so doing, we can build strong solid relationships that last a lifetime. The skills required to build good solid relationships are referred to as 'soft people skills', and they are highly sought after in any environment where there is a gathering of people. If we want to excel as leaders, a critical skill requirement is 'people skills'. Leadership is about influence, not dictatorship, and without great soft skills we will fail in this area.

Teachers are very important in our lives and we need to value them, cooperate with them and respect them highly indeed. A teacher's responsibility is to help us develop and increase our ability to reach our potential. Sometimes, this means challenging and pushing us to our limits so that we can reach higher levels and achieve great things that we may have thought were impossible.

Education teaches us to be independent. Being independent means we learn to trust our instincts and frames of reference to make the right decisions at the right time. It helps us to make good decisions based on intuition, reasoning and logic rather than just accepting situations or what anyone tells us.

Learning to manage our time is an invaluable skill which is required in all parts of our life. Education offers us several opportunities to develop this skill with assignment deadlines, combined with balancing family and possible work responsibilities. Managing our variety of activities and time requires discipline, and there's no better place to learn discipline than in formal education because very quickly we recognise that every action has a consequence. From missing deadlines to passing exams, we learn to deal with the consequences of our actions. As such, being organised is key to our success in every area of our lives. We will struggle to excel in our education if we can't plan and make the time to deliver our assignments as well as balance our social life alongside our studies.

Finally, during our education we will have the opportunity to be exposed to many different fields of work and this gives us the opportunity to choose fields that we are passionate about as we plan our careers. In my experience, there are two types of education: formal education (which incorporates academic and vocational) and life-skills education, both of which are equally important to survive in this world.

ACADEMIC EDUCATION

Academic education is the formal education system we are all aware of, relating to a school, academy, college or other educational institution, especially one for higher education. The subjects taught are generic and include English, maths, sciences, history, geography, art and foreign languages. These subjects give us the foundation to branch out into specific career paths.

VOCATIONAL EDUCATION

Vocational education prepares people to work in a specific trade or a craft, such as becoming a technician, or in professional vocations such as engineering, accountancy, nursing, medicine, architecture or law. Craft vocations are usually based on manual or practical activities and are traditionally non-academic, being instead related to a specific trade or occupation. Vocational education is sometimes referred to as career education or technical education.

LIFE SKILLS EDUCATION

'Life skills' are the flexible abilities for positive behaviour that enable us to deal effectively with the demands and challenges of everyday life. There is no definitive list of life skills, but some of the skill areas include: attitudes, values, behaviours, decision-making, goal-setting, problem-solving, coping with stress, coping with emotions, negotiating, friendship, interpersonal relationships, confidence, communication skills, people skills, empathy (concern for others), critical thinking, creative thinking, resisting peer pressure, assertiveness and resolving conflict.

Until recently, not much focus has been given to the importance of life skills education and yet research has proven that our success in life is dependent on these skills after we have acquired academic or vocational education. After acquiring a skill and knowledge, our level of success in any chosen career path is dependent on our life skills. Some of the tools acquired from this book will help increase your life skills to make you more successful.

Bringing Education to Life in the Theatre of Life

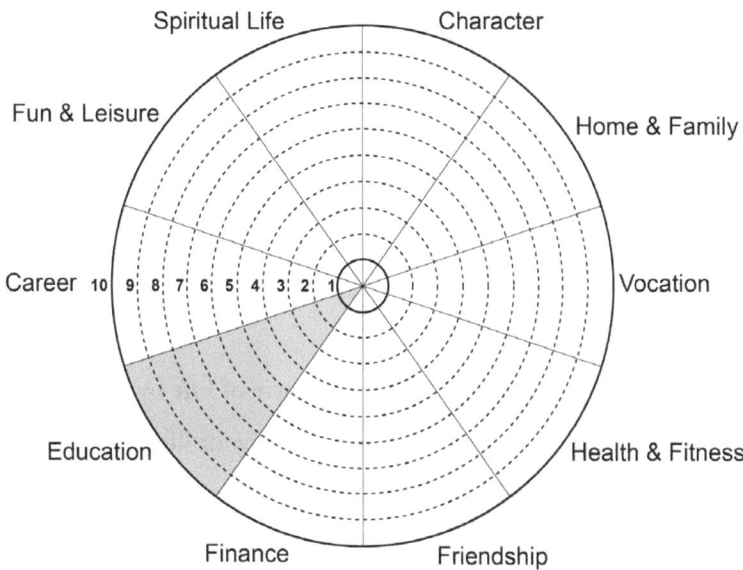

Know Thyself

The first place to begin on a life-long journey of education is to identify where you currently are in the area of your education. Tate your satisfaction level by placing a mark on the wheel. Point 10 represents very satisfied and Point 0 represents very dissatisfied.

Now recognise that you will forever keep learning – either through life experiences or through academic pursuits.

Make the Commitment

Depending on the score you gave yourself, begin to think about increasing your score to educate yourself further by:

1. Recognising the importance of this area and the difference
    it will make in your life. How would you like to see yourself
    behaving once this area of your life has been satisfied?
    What would your life look like? What would your
    relationships look like? How would this impact your world
    professionally and socially?

2. You can choose to research, learn or read more about it.
    Recommended reading to improve life skills: the Bible,
    How to Win Friends and Influence People by Dale
    Carnegie, and Seven Habits of Highly Effective People by
    Stephen Covey.

Finally, bring that area into the Theatre of Life by:

1. Defining your desire for this area of your life.

2. Writing it down in detail, in positive language as though it
    has already happened.

3. Meditating (visualising) on what you have written.

4. Speaking out what you have written with confidence, as
    though it has already happened.

5. Thanking God for providing your heart's desire.

6. Go to work: apply what you have learnt from this book and
    from other resources – practise, practise, practise!

Chapter 10

CAREER PLANNING

"Whoever refuses to work is not allowed to eat."
2 Thessalonians 3:10 (GNT)

"If you used to rob, you must stop robbing and start working, in order to earn an honest living for yourself and to be able to help the poor." Ephesians 4:28 (GNT)

Clearly, God takes working seriously and recognises that it is a very important aspect of our life journey. From the above scriptures it is obvious that working is default to our existence. Consider this, though: we have twenty-four hours in a day and we spend around eight hours sleeping and approximately twelve hours working, inclusive of travel. In other words, we spend a significant portion of our time working, so it is very important that we enjoy what we do if we want to live happy lives.

The majority of the world's population is doing jobs that they hate. Out of desperation or necessity we take any job that will help us pay our bills, support our families and live a particular lifestyle. The job may not always be terrible, but it offers us very little real satisfaction. It is admirable that we find a job to pay our own way and support our families, and although we may start off this way, it does not have to stay like this. No matter where we are in life right now, we can begin to plan a career in line with our gifts, skills and abilities so we can enjoy a fulfilling life journey. Whether we are a school student, a school leaver, an adult focused on adding new skills, or an adult focused on changing a job or career, it is never too late to plan a career path or a change in career direction.

One thing is certain regarding career planning, and this is 'change'. We should be willing to embrace ongoing change because the process of discovering our gifts, skills and abilities (vocation or calling) is a journey of discovery, and this influences our career decisions over the years ahead. Equally, due to the ever-changing nature of the job market, economies and society in general, career planning should be an ongoing process and this will help to direct our learning and development. We are ultimately responsible for our own careers, so the process begins with us – not with our parents, family members, friends, bosses or careers services.

PLOT THE JOURNEY

The first place to begin on the career-planning journey is to identify our gifts, skills, abilities (calling), interests, values, and other priorities in life including areas of our lives outside of work. The chapter on Vocation in this book will be very helpful for this exercise. We can't start mapping our career route if we don't have this information.

The next step is to identify where we want to go. We need a destination point to help us plot our career path. Due to the changing nature of life, we may keep adjusting the destination point as the months and years roll on. We may choose to have several particular destination points, as we set goals for the short term, medium term and long term. Once we have a clear vision of where we want to be in the next one, two, five and ten years we can construct a road map to get there.

We can begin by asking ourselves several questions:

- Where am I now?

- Where do I want to be and when do I want to get there?

- What do I want out of a job or career? (location, hours of work, benefits, home working, self-employment, work/life balance)

- What is important to me?

When plotting our future, rather than focusing on companies and positions, it is more important to think about the skills and expertise necessary to achieve our dream career. While we cannot control whether we will be hired at a specific organisation, we can position ourselves to be a top candidate for exciting jobs by equipping ourselves with a great CV.

EXPLORE OCCUPATIONS

At this point, we are ready to explore various occupations and learn about areas that might interest us. Once we have some idea of the occupations that appeal to us, we can investigate the specific skills and qualifications required to work in those fields. As we explore these occupations, we can ask ourselves questions such as:

- Do my skills match up with the requirements of these occupations?

- Do these occupations align with my interests and gifts/calling?

- What skills do I need?

- What skills am I lacking?

- How do I equip myself with the necessary skills or qualifications to plug any gaps?

- Where do I find work in my chosen occupation/s?

- How would this occupation fit in with my current situation and responsibilities?

- What adjustments would I have to make to my current lifestyle to accommodate my chosen occupation?

- What are the advantages and disadvantages for each option?

The internet is a great resource for researching an exhaustive list of hundreds of career options.

TAKE ACTION

Let's start plotting each step we need to put our plan into action. We have now gathered a lot of information about the areas of work that align with our gifts, skills, abilities, interests and values in order to create our plan.

We can now consider the following:

- What action can I take right now that will help me move closer to my chosen occupation, training and career goals?

- Do I need external help and if so, where can I get this help?

- Who in my network of support can assist me?

- What other steps can I take? Work experience, work shadowing or more research?

- Where can I find job opportunities and apply for them?

WHERE TO FIND JOBS

The majority of jobs are not always advertised so we have to broaden our search to cover all areas including the 'hidden job market', as described in John Lees' book How to Get a Job You'll Love.

Let's look at some of the options available to find work:

- Word-of-mouth connections

- Recommendations by colleagues or friends

- Direct approach to individuals or companies

- Volunteer work

- Temporary positions
- Part-time/job share
- Apprenticeships
- Job advertisements: newspapers, industry magazines, company websites
- Private employment agencies: recruitment consultants
- Job centres
- Internet searches / online job boards by employers and agencies
- Social media

CONSTRUCTING A WINNING CV

CV stands for curriculum vitae, which is Latin for 'course of life'. It is a summary of our experience, skills and education. Our CV is usually our first point of contact with a potential employer. It is the first opportunity we get to make a good impression. First impressions have a long-lasting impact on people's minds and since competition in the marketplace is fierce, we need to take the time to put together a great and memorable CV. On average a CV is read in under twenty seconds, and this means the first few paragraphs on the first page must work really hard to get us the desired attention. There are different ways of setting out a CV depending on your work experience, achievements, the position you are applying for, and the impact or impression you want to make. As such, it is worth researching this topic for guidance or seeking help from people who have great experience in this area.

As part of your research on writing a winning CV, I highly recommend a book by John Lees, called How to Get a Job You'll Love. This book is very comprehensive and covers almost every angle of career planning, including great tips on designing a good CV, interview techniques and job-searching techniques.

SUCCESS STORIES

To help inspire you to achieve great success in your careers, I am indebted to the eighteen great minds who took the time to share their life stories with me.

The late Earl Nightingale, a self-help speaker and author, defines success as 'the progressive realisation of a worthy goal'.

This means that anyone who is on course toward the fulfilment of a goal is successful and it gives me huge pleasure to share with you the life experiences of eighteen very successful people in the United Kingdom. I had the good fortune of interviewing these great minds, and their stories shed some valuable insights which will help us greatly in our own pursuits.

Below is a collective summary of the interviews, organised into ten themes:

1. Childhood Experiences

Do childhood experiences have an impact on the person we become? Absolutely! Whilst positive experiences can provide the building blocks to success, negative experiences can also spur people on to accomplish great things.

One key lesson that I learnt from tapping into the minds of these great thinkers was that, whatever positive or negative experiences they had, they chose how each experience would impact them – as a hindrance or an opportunity – and used the experience to their advantage.

How does this apply to you? Whatever your experiences have been to date, only YOU can choose how they affect you. Are they stepping stones to becoming the person you are destined to be; or hurdles to be overcome?

Your thinking, speaking and environment (either positive or negative) will determine the type of outcome you achieve.

Let's look at some of the experiences shared by the interviewees on their childhood:

Positive Experiences	Negative Experiences	Bittersweet Experiences
Both parents in a loving environment	Being bullied	Parents divorcing
Parents financially stable	Parents brought up in poverty	Parent(s) dying
Secure family background		Away from family in early years (boarding school)
Strong father figure; challenged and encouraged not to settle for the status quo	Parent(s) dealing with addictions	Parents' successful business failing due to recession
Supportive, stable home	Grew up in a ghetto	Completed university degree as an adult
Hardworking and disciplined parents	Little or no parental guidance or encouragement	
Stable childhood		
Very happy childhood		

So, as we ponder on the range of experiences above, let's ask ourselves these questions:

1. How can we change our experiences to our advantage?

2. What changes do we need to make in the way we think about our experiences?

3. How can we change our current environment?

(HINT – two key words appear in the above questions: 'change' and 'think'.)

Excerpts from the Interviews on Childhood:

- 'Basically, I had a secure family background, and if you are loved as a child it is a great support.'

- 'A stable and happy childhood is an amazing platform to make your way in life. Although my parents got divorced, I am of the view that great parenting can be done even with a split family.'

- 'I did not get any encouragement from my parents as a youngster, but then again, I was in the same situation as all the kids I knew and went to school with.'

- 'Being the youngest child, and quite often ignored by siblings, makes you want to prove something. I was mostly quiet among my siblings but I was quietly planning.'

2. Developing Disciplines

The word discipline means: 'training expected to produce a specific character or pattern of behaviour, especially training that produces moral or mental improvement.' (Free Dictionary.com)

To challenge ourselves even further, let us ask ourselves this question: can we begin to develop habits that will train us to produce a specific character/pattern/behaviour to bring about a desired outcome? It's never too late to develop a new discipline – in fact, we just developed one by changing the way we think about our experiences! You are your own Boss, so 'Tame Your Boss' to cultivate discipline.

Let us review the interviewees' experiences relating to developing disciplines:

Discipline Developed	Impact
Running/jogging	• Built self-confidence • Encouragement to train harder and win more trophies. • Maintain healthy mind and body • Learn to be competitive
Reading	• Obtained knowledge and understanding of the world around me, relevant to work
Independent thinking	• Being organised • Not being influenced by peers • Follow own path • Develop a set of values that was not shared by peers or environment
Strong work ethic	• Greater returns in life depending on the efforts put in – consistently and routinely • Provides the means to look after yourself • Understand responsibility
Religion	• Here to serve others

Excerpts on Discipline:

- 'There is a quote that says that anything achieved easily is not worthy of attainment. So, all the best things you have achieved in life, you have had to work for.'

- 'I know that in life you can be average at something, but if you work really hard at it, you can be one of the best.'

- 'I never really had any habits or disciplines. I was just a complete scatty and untidy and disorganised twit. However, when I came into the work force I realised that you have got to be disciplined and very organised.'

- 'One of the habits I developed very early, and perhaps a lot earlier than most people my age, was that you had to get up early and work hard, and you have to do that consistently and routinely in order to progress.'

3. Sources of Inspiration and Influence

We are all influenced and inspired by many things around us: what we watch, see and hear. Positive influences can act as a catalyst for discovering our potential – the greatness hidden inside us. What has 'sparked' your interest lately? Was it something you read, a song you heard or an experience shared? Let's look at the impact of some of the influences that acted as a spark/catalyst for the great minds we are studying.

Influence / Source of Inspiration	Impact
Religion and family values	Kept me on the straight and narrow
Teacher	Source of inspiration outside of family circle
Being part of a group	Provided the confidence to challenge the status quo
Commanding Officer	Taught me to surround myself with people who are the best of the best – and very often that means they are better than you
Head Teacher	Great role model; inspired us to go out and achieve great things
History teacher	Taught me how to analyse, to be objective and not subjective, how to write an essay, how to draw information together and consolidate it

Excerpts on Influences / Sources of Inspiration:

- 'The powerful influence which helped turn things around for me was my family and the values they instilled in me.'

- 'I attended a day school which wasn't really good and my parents saw that I wasn't really learning anything, so they took me out and sent me to a guy who is a remarkable teacher. He was an amazing man – taught ten kids in his front room on all subjects.'

- 'Sometimes people need an example that you can copy, or somebody with wise words.'

- 'History as a subject teaches you how to think, how to analyse, how to be objective and not subjective, how to write an essay, how to draw information together and consolidate it. And this is what my history teacher did really well at.'

- 'I often wonder if my son is being taught well enough on how to learn. Loads of information is dumped on them but are the teachers spending enough time with them to help them think it through.'

4. The Importance of Reading

In his book Think Big, Dr Ben Carson emphasises that the student who excels academically reads extensively, and that there is a correlation between avid readers and intellectual accomplishments.

In this same book, Carson cites a quote by Aldous Huxley which reads, 'Every man who knows how to read has it in his power to magnify himself, to multiply the ways in which he exists, to make his life full, significant, and interesting'.

Earl Nightingale, author of Lead the Field, also stresses that 'a person who does not read is no better than one who cannot read'.

So, in carrying on with the theme of influences, how do you think these great thinkers rate reading – high or low? Let's find out.

Avid Reader	Books Read
Yes	The Bible, Guinness World Book of Records
Yes	1984 (George Orwell), Investment Biker (Jim Rogers)
Yes	Man's Search for Meaning (Viktor Frankl)
Yes	Biographies (e.g. of Abraham Lincoln) and autobiographies
Yes	The novels of Charles Dickens
Yes	Survival of The Fittest (Sir Ranulph Fiennes and Mike Stroud), Touching the Void (Joe Simpson), Lords of Finance (Liaquat Ahamed)
Yes	Historical books

Excerpts on Reading:

- 'Reading used to be a job; it is now a pleasure.'

- 'I cannot recall my parents sitting down with me and talking through morals, etc.; they always gave me books.'

- 'In my younger days I read a lot of books. At one stage I was reading six books a week. I was a very fast reader and I have got books and books and books around the house. I now read one or possibly two books a month.'

- 'I find the books that I read add to my life skills.'

- 'My reading has contributed to who I am today.'

- 'Reading is very important, but I would say, for young people, read anything – anything that takes you away from the TV.'

5. People – The Company We Keep

Are we defined by the company we keep? Oh yes!! A great writer, Paul of Tarsus, once wrote that 'bad company corrupts good character'. And to quote Benjamin Franklin, 'be slow in choosing a friend, and slower in changing'.

Quite literally, we become (over time) the company we keep. So we must ask ourselves if the company we are keeping is helping or preventing us from reaching our goals.

During the interviews, I asked these great minds if they surrounded themselves with particular kinds of people. Let's find out some of their responses.

Types of People	Why
People who view the bottle as half full and not half empty	They have an enthusiasm about life
People who have strong family values	Do not like social climbers
Authentic people	I want to have an honest open heart-to-heart conversation
People with good energy, open-minded, flexible in terms of the way they think	Usually have nice personalities and are enthusiastic
People from different walks of life	You learn a lot more from different types of people
People who are different to me	More stimulating to have a mix of thought processes or approaches
Intellectually stimulating	Interested in how things work

Excerpts on People:

- 'I do not spend time with negative people. I find positive people with a natural love of life very good for the soul.'

- 'A long time ago a family friend told me we can put people in one of two categories, and he used the term 'drains' or 'radiators'. The 'drains' are the people who suck the energy out of you with their complaining, etc., and you do not like being with them because you feel uncomfortable with them. Then you get the people who are the 'radiators'. As soon as they walk into the room, most of them smile; they have bright eyes and they have a wonderful energy.'

6. Toolkit for Success

In planning our journey to success, there are many factors to consider. For example, we may consider developing our own blueprint for success. However, let's consider the different tools/principles used by those who have experienced success:

Tools	Why
Family and health	Produces energy and enthusiasm for life and work
Put your client first	By consistently delivering what the client needs, things just seem to fall into place
Ability to visualise or imagine things	If you dream it often enough, it can happen
Think for yourself	To be able to evaluate things for yourself before making decisions

Excerpts on Tools for Success:

- 'You need lots of desire and commitment and it is good to have good mentors to direct you.'

- 'Motivation is quite intrinsic. You need to find what it is that makes you tick and you need to place yourself in an environment that gives you that.'

- 'It is important to have the desire to do whatever it is you want to do to the very best of your ability, and to do it honestly.'

- 'Clarity – looking at things clearly e.g. if you are bogged down with the detail you have to step back and look at it in a more panoramic perspective to put things into context.'

7. Dealing with Rejection/Failure

The journey to success is littered with many pitstops of rejection and failure. However, successful people view these failures as open doors to new opportunities. Henry Ford, the founder of Ford Motor Company, once said, 'Failure is simply an opportunity to begin again, this time more intelligently'.

Here are some great hints and tips on how these great thinkers dealt with rejection/failure:

- 'If I fail at something, I don't take it well and it makes me want to fight back even more. If one fails in life, it can be a priceless lesson. So you can't sit there and cry: ask yourself where you went wrong. Use it as a case study to ensure you don't repeat those mistakes again.'

- 'People say that you always learn more from your mistakes than your successes.'

- 'I take it on the chin. I read somewhere that the definition of success is: Falling seven times and getting up eight times. I try to look at lessons learnt in any difficult situation.'

- 'I would say being prepared to stick it out. A key to success is just to keep on turning up. So many people give up.'

- 'You have got to move on. You can either take it personally and emotionally and get really depressed about it, or wipe it from your mind and move on to the next thing.'

- 'It just revs me up again. If I fail or make a mistake, I just want to come back fighting. If I lose, I want to win even more. It does not drive me to distraction. When you are young and make mistakes it really annoys you, but as you get older, you are a bit more pragmatic about it. I have always got the fight to want to win again.'

- 'One has to build resilience to persevere. I suppose also humility is a great thing, because sometimes you think you're that great, but actually you are not.'

8. Priorities that Govern Your Life

In the hugely successful book by Steven Covey called Seven Habits of Highly Effective People, the third habit is 'Put first things first'. Successful people develop a code / set of rules that they govern their lives by.

How do you go about doing this? Let's look at these great minds as a frame of reference:

- '"Pre-Planning and Preparation Prevents Poor Performance." This was an old army expression and is incredibly important for everything.'

- 'Firstly, my family, the health of myself and my family, my work, my friends, my faith.'

- 'Stay healthy – because without your health everything falls apart. Keep your family together – that's important because a lot flows from that. Keep learning – keep challenging yourself. Set yourself new challenges so that you don't get complacent. If you sit there doing the same thing and don't challenge yourself, the brain does not develop. Slow down, take your time but don't waste time.'

- 'Being a good parent. Being authentic and staying true to myself. Being mindful and sensitive to the feelings of others. Striking a balance between following my path without sacrificing myself for the sake of others, and without hurting others.'

- 'Belief in something. Contributing to people's lives. Family. Balance in life. Constant renewal – new year, new challenges. Keep learning.'

- 'The first would be doing right. I think that is enormously important. The second thing is being generous and helpful to others if you possibly can. Honesty is also incredibly important, and then giving your best and wanting to feel that you have tried as hard as you can.'

- 'God, the family, honesty, fairness.'

- 'Provide for my family – very important. Educate my children. Trying to do the best with what I have been given. Also, to improve other people's lives.'

9. Words of Wisdom

As a special gift to us, each interviewee provided a number of signposts based on their experiences to help us to develop our own personal road map to success and I have shared a few below:

Signpost 1

'Get to know yourself. Be honest with yourself. Try and get on with your fellow human beings because if you do they will help you and you can help them. If you have had a tough time in life, you can either let it get you down or use it as fuel to move you forward.'

Signpost 2

'Listen to your heart, follow your passion and follow it absolutely and wholeheartedly. Do not be scared to make mistakes; keep learning from each mistake. Keep going.'

Signpost 3

'Be bold. Believe in yourself – in the right way. Amazing things can happen if you have the right foundation and do things right. Be confident about what you are doing.'

Signpost 4

'Belief in yourself is absolutely crucial. When somebody is selling a product, they have to have confidence. They can only have confidence if they really believe in what they are selling. In life, you are selling yourself – whether you are going for a job or trying to sell someone a product etc. You can only do that if you have self-belief. '

'Think hard. There is a quote by someone called Russell in the early 1900s, and the quote is: 'most people think once or twice a year; I have made a career for myself thinking once or twice a week'. Never underestimate the power of thinking for yourself.'

'Work hard. You really have to have a strong work ethic – but with a balance of up time and down time.'

Signpost 5

'Be aware of what you are good at and the things you struggle with. Learn to work with your strengths and weaknesses. Treat people with respect and in the way that you want to be treated. Never be afraid of failure; never let it defeat you.'

Signpost 6

'Do what you love and what you enjoy. Do not do things that you think can earn you a lot of money – this can lead to unhappiness and heartache. Be honest, be credible – people will see right through you if you are dishonest. Remember, it takes years to build a good name and it can take an instant to demolish it. Be nice, be outgoing. Surround yourself with good people. Love your family. Be conscientious with your family. Finally, work hard, have a very good work ethic and have a passion for reading and acquiring information .'

Signpost 7

'The word most people will use to describe how they have achieved is the word "luck". Luck comes at a price, and the price of luck is hard work. In trying to find your niche, you will have to work very hard – which will involve overcoming disappointments. But when you find your niche, be brave enough to make whatever changes are needed.

Strive to be the best; use every opportunity to gain work experience / employment in your chosen company / profession. Charm the people you work with – be memorable. You have a product to sell, and that product is you.

Signpost 8

'Be patient in your career. Be prepared to stand against the crowd – to go your own way if you have to. Be helpful to others and don't get discouraged if things are not going right.'

Signpost 9

'Make a plan. Stick to your plan and do not be distracted. Continue to practise, practise, practise – sharpening your skills and experience. Don't be surprised if things to go wrong or you experience setbacks – you have to keep on going and push harder.'

Signpost 10

'Set targets and review them on a yearly basis. Work out / plan how you are going to achieve them and achieve them! Build a step-by-step picture of your life.'

Signpost 11

'Be scrupulously honest. Be prepared to keep your own counsel. Do what you want to do and do this to the best of your ability.

'A parting word of advice that I also shared with my youngest son – a quote Eleanor Roosevelt (former First Lady of the USA): "No one can make you feel inferior without your permission". So, if your boss doesn't think you are good at your job, take action, and go and find another job if necessary.'

Signpost 12

'Be enthusiastic, be curious, be inquisitive, ever wanting to learn – listen to other people to learn. Be humble and never give up. There is no excuse for being bored – you must develop an attitude of curiosity and inquisitiveness. Don't worry about what other people think, get on with it. Don't try and make money for the sake of making money. You must do what you enjoy doing.'

Signpost 13

'Keep on learning. All your life you have to keep learning because there is so much to learn. Remain open to new ideas; recognise opportunities – look out for them, apply patience and work hard. The more you put into something, the more you get out of it.

'We all think that we want to be happy, but actually what we really want is to be fulfilled. You can't do that by resting on your laurels; it's hard work. We have to try and overcome challenges, and until we do that, we are never fulfilled.

10. A Final Word on Discovering Potential

I hope that the words captured in this section have sparked something inside you, to inspire and encourage you to keep on pursuing the person who you are meant to become – a person of purpose. No matter what your situation, background or academic position is, everyone has a 'pivotal moment' in their lives that acts as a catalyst to discovering their potential.

Let's take a look at someone who had their 'pivotal moment':

'I was never an academic and was very lazy in school. I did not want to learn about academia and was always bottom of the class in most subjects. Sixth Form was a wake-up call for me, as I was put into a group of bright academic children from good homes. Over time, I realised that I had an interest in finance, and I began to develop a passion for reading history on finance, traders etc…

'I just about got the grades to get into university to study Economics and Finance. After graduating, I undertook a temporary role in the City for about six months. It was during this period I realised that I had some capabilities. I realised that I wasn't as stupid as I thought I was.'

Bringing Career Planning to Life in the Theatre of Life

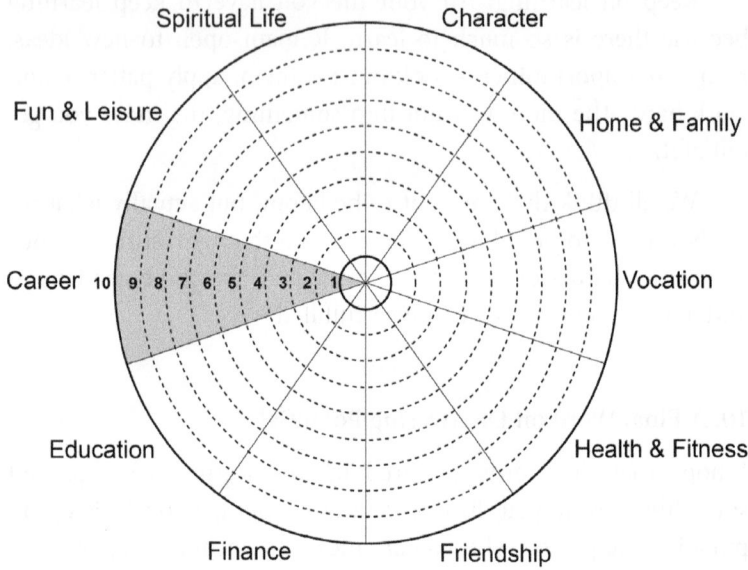

Know Thyself

Now, to identify where you currently are in the area of your career, rate your satisfaction level by placing a mark on the wheel. Point 10 represents very satisfied and Point 0 represents very dissatisfied.

Fix the Destination

Next, get to the root of the problem. If you are currently working, does your current job fit your skills and abilities? Are you doing this role out of necessity or for the money? If you are not currently working, what career would you like to pursue and how would it affect your life? To help, we can ask ourselves several questions:

- Am I happy in the role I am doing now?

- Do I live for the weekends?

- What makes me feel alive, that I can do for hours and not realise that time has gone by?

Make the Commitment

Depending on the score you gave yourself, begin to think about increasing your score to build a better career by:

1. Recognising the importance of this area and the difference it will make in your life. How would you like to see yourself behaving once this area of your life has been satisfied? What would your life look like? What would your relationships look like? How would this impact your world professionally and socially?

2. You can choose to research, learn or read more about it.

Finally, bring that area into the Theatre of Life by:

1. Defining your desire for this area of your life.

2. Writing it down in detail, in positive language as though it has already happened.

3. Meditating (visualising) on what you have written.

4. Speaking out what you have written with confidence, as though it has already happened.

5. Thanking God for providing your heart's desire.

6. Go to work: apply what you have learnt from this book and from other resources – practise, practise, practise!

Chapter 11

FUN AND LEISURE

"Here is what I have found out: the best thing we can do is eat and drink and enjoy what we have worked for during the short life that God has given us; this is our fate. If God gives us wealth and property and lets us enjoy them, we should be grateful and enjoy what we have worked for. It is a gift from God." Ecclesiastes 5:18-19 (GNT)

Dictionary.com describes *'leisure'* as: *'time free from the demands of work or duty, when one can rest, enjoy hobbies or sports, etc.'*

The positive effects of leisure and recreation on people is the subject of a great deal of research because of the overall benefits to both a stable functioning society and productivity in the workplace. Research suggests that leisure activities have more impact on a person's quality of life than any other aspect of experience and behaviour.

There are several benefits of leisure activities such as mental and physical health, family bonding, environmental benefits and economic development, which explains the reason why many countries including the United Kingdom are encouraging participation in leisure activities.

Leisure is essential to our well-being. When we have positive feelings of self-esteem and a sense of control or understanding of our life, we are much happier, more productive and fun to be with.

By taking our minds off the pressures and demands of everyday life, at work or in school, leisure helps us eliminate stress.

'All work and no play makes Jack a dull boy'. This is especially true as studies have revealed that people who take time to unwind through leisure and recreational activities tend to be more fulfilled in their personal lives than those who don't. Child psychologists also recommend plenty of play for children. Leisure and recreation help improve our mood.

There are two types of leisure activities: 'active' leisure and 'passive' leisure. Active leisure relates to physical activities such as singing, playing an instrument, or doing exercise or sports. Passive leisure relates to things such as reading, watching television, listening to music or hanging out with friends. Both types of leisure activities have advantages and typically a balance between the two is most beneficial.

Active leisure can have a positive effect on physical health, emotional health, and the health of our social relationships. When considering the benefits of the different types of leisure activities, it is important to consider some activities that relate to the development of a specific skill or ability. These activities require effort and persistence and very often give us an opportunity to enhance our drive and motivation as well as giving us a sense of fulfilment and achievement. Active leisure is beneficial to our health because it helps us relax by improving blood circulation throughout the body. It also helps us to burn calories and thereby manage our weight.

Participating in leisure activities helps us understand ourselves better and increases our awareness of our bodies, which is important for our well-being. The social aspects of leisure activities can give us a sense of belonging, which also helps to boost our self-esteem. As such, group activities and team sports are perfect to develop our social skills, values, integrity and attitudes, and to build strong character.

Making time for a balance of work, play and leisure is not easy. Relationships with others, both at work and in our personal life, are an integral part of how we manage and enjoy life. Nurturing and fostering interpersonal relationships takes time and energy and at times we may feel fragmented or overwhelmed if we are not achieving a sense of balance. Our work and relationships will suffer if we are not managing to meet our needs and responsibilities, in addition to considering the needs of others at our workplace and in our personal life.

Even if we love our work immensely, we need to remember that it is only a part of our life. To lead a well-balanced life, we should have interests outside work. Indulging in these activities also reduces stress and makes us develop a positive attitude toward life. Relaxation and fun need to be permanent parts of our lives – they make our lives more fulfilling.

A list of some different leisure activities for you and your family/friends to consider:

Sport and Physical Recreation

- Solo activities – gym or swimming
- Group activities – team games

Arts and Entertainment

- Theatre
- Concerts
- Comedy clubs
- Films

Countryside Recreation

- Hiking
- Camping
- Picnics

- Cycling
- Youth hostelling
- Horse riding

Home-Based Leisure

- Reading
- Make-overs
- Gardening
- TV, Internet
- Computer games and Online gaming

Visitor Attractions

- Theme and leisure parks
- Museums
- Historic buildings

Catering

- Fast-food restaurants
- Cafes
- Pub restaurants
- Top restaurants

Bringing Fun and Leisure to Life in the Theatre of Life

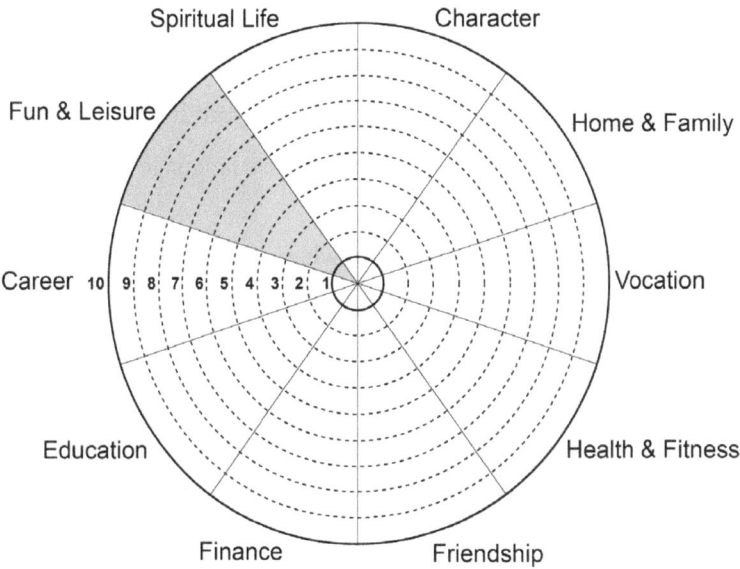

Know Thyself

Now we want to identify where we currently are in the area of Fun and Leisure. Rate your satisfaction level by placing a mark on the wheel. Point 10 represents very satisfied and Point 0 represents very dissatisfied.

Make the Commitment

Depending on the score you gave yourself, begin to think about increasing your score to build a better Fun and Leisure life by:

1. Recognising the importance of this area and the difference it will make in your life. How would you like to see yourself behaving once this area of your life has been satisfied? What would your life look like? What would your

relationships look like? How would this impact your world professionally and socially?

2.   You can choose to research, learn or read more about it.

Finally, bring that area into the Theatre of Life by:

1.   Defining your desire for this area of your life.

2.   Writing it down in detail, in positive language as though it has already happened.

3.   Meditating (visualising) on what you have written.

4.   Speaking out what you have written with confidence, as though it has already happened.

5.   Thanking God for providing your heart's desire.

6.   Go to work: apply what you have learnt from this book and from other resources – practise, practise, practise!

Chapter 12

SPIRITUAL LIFE

When we are born, we start our life journey by seeking fulfilment. We begin our life journey by looking to our mother and father for fulfilment: from food, clothing and shelter through to companionship (connecting with other people). As we get older, we continue to seek fulfilment from the same things but the list begins to expand. Sooner rather than later, we realise that money is key to acquiring majority of our material needs, so then we begin to pursue money through work by acquiring a skill which we trade in exchange for money.

Throughout this life journey our desire for fulfilment from material things and companionship begins to increase, yet the more we get, the more we want, because we are still not completely fulfilled. Somehow, there is a never-ending void or gap in our hearts which still needs filling. There are times when, despite all the material things we accumulate and all the companionship we have, we still feel a sense of emptiness. I am convinced that the emptiness or void we feel can only be filled by God, our manufacturer. God, who is a Spirit, created us in his image and likeness – spirit, first and foremost, so that we can have a relationship with Him just as a child would have with a father. The void we feel is specific to our spirit-man and only the spirit-of-God can fulfil that.

God is seeking a wonderful and close relationship with us. When we don't have a relationship with God, there is a tendency to pursue life alone. For long periods in my life I pursued life alone until the going got really tough, and there comes a time in everyone's life when we all have to deal with difficult challenges. Sometimes we have to face certain challenges alone whether we like it or not, because depending on the situation, either no one is in a position to help or no one is willing to help. As the saying goes, you find yourself between a rock and a hard place. It is usually at this point that most people are open to seeking help from a God who is compassionate and merciful, and for me, this was the case.

In addition to this, there are times when we seek comfort to ease a burden but we lack the insight or wisdom to make the right decision. A relationship with God can provide us with the deep inner comfort we need or can provide us with the divine wisdom we need to make the right choices. Once I discovered God, my life began to make sense and to take on a more purposeful direction. The void I felt disappeared. I had a level of comfort and peace that I had never experienced before. When I experienced challenges, I did not have to face them alone and it was of great comfort to know that God had my back and could provide me with guidance when I needed it most.

My relationship with God gave me a sense of quiet confidence and assurance that can only be received by knowing God. Knowing God completed my life because He makes provision for every area of my life. Without God, it is possible to make all the money we want, and to buy all the material things we want, but that approach may come with distress, grief, sadness or regret. However, the Bible says: *"The blessing of the Lord makes one rich, And He adds no sorrow with it."* (Proverbs 10:22). There are also things in life that money can't buy and when that situation presents itself, we find ourselves unable to deal with it. For example, when our relationships with friends, family or colleagues begin to fail, or our loved ones begin to experience health challenges that money can't fix, what do we do then?

God's provision covers every area of our lives, from finances through to our work, health, relationships and recreation. And our lives feel more complete once we have a relationship with Him. So what does it take to begin a relationship with God? God has made it very clear in the Bible how we can know Him. Because God created us and loves us so much, He wants us to know Him personally and to spend the rest of our lives with Him, here on earth and even beyond. Jesus said: *"For God so loved the world that he gave his only Son so that everyone who believes in Him will not perish but have eternal life."* (John 3:16)

Jesus came to our world so each of us could know and understand God in a personal way. Only Jesus can bring meaning and purpose to our life. However, during our relationship with God, we can sometimes sense a distance from Him. This can be due to many reasons, but one of them can be due to our sin. Sin is simply doing what is wrong or not doing what is right according to God's rules. Sin causes a spiritual separation from God (spiritual death). Although we may try to get close to God through doing good for others, religious rituals, trying to be a good person, etc, these do not work because none of these good efforts actually cover up our sin or remove it.

God is holy and therefore cannot connect with sin. As such, our sin prevents us from having a relationship with God. Because of His tremendous love for us, God put a great plan in place to fix the sin situation so that we can have a loving relationship with Him. The great plan was to send Jesus into our world to take on our sins (exchanging our sins with holiness) so that we can appear before Him sinless and blameless and have a strong deep relationship with Him.

The great news is that Jesus Christ took away all our sins – everything we have ever done and everything we will ever do in the future. He personally paid for them with His life by suffering and dying on the cross. He died in our place out of His tremendous love for us. Because of Jesus' death on the cross, our sin doesn't have to separate us from God any longer.

"For God loved the world so much that he gave his only Son, so that everyone who believes in Him may not die but have eternal life." John 3:16 (GNB)

Jesus not only died for our sins, He rose from the dead. When He did, He proved beyond doubt that He can rightfully promise eternal life, that He is the Son of God and the only means by which we can know God. That is why Jesus said: *"I am the way, the truth, and the life; no one goes to the Father except by me."* Instead of trying harder to reach God, Jesus tells us how we can begin a relationship with Him right now. Jesus says: *"Come to me... If anyone thirsts, let him come to me and drink. Whoever believes in me... out of his heart will flow rivers of living water."* It was Jesus' love for us that caused him to suffer on the cross, and he now invites us to come to Him, that we might begin a personal relationship with God.

Just knowing what Jesus has done for us and what He is offering us is not enough. To have a relationship with God, we need to welcome Him into our life. The Bible says: *"Yet to all who received Him, to those who believed in His name, He gave the right to become children of God."* We accept Jesus by faith. The Bible says: *"God saved you by His special favour when you believed. And you can't take credit for this; it is a gift from God. Salvation is not a reward for the good things we have done, so none of us can boast about it."* Accepting Jesus means believing that He is the Son of God, who He claimed to be, then inviting Him to guide and direct our lives. Jesus said: I came that you might have life, and have it more abundantly.

So here is the invitation from Jesus. He said: *"I'm standing at the door and I'm knocking. If anyone hears my voice and opens the door, I will come in."* Would you like to respond to His invitation? Here's how. The precise words you use to commit yourself to God are not important. He knows the intentions of your heart. If you are unsure of what to pray, this might help you put it into words:

Jesus, I want to know you. I want you to come into my life. Thank you for dying on the cross for my sin so that I could be fully accepted by God. Only you can give me the power to change and become the person you created me to be. Thank you for forgiving me and giving me eternal life with God. I give my life to you. Please do with it as you wish. Amen.

If you sincerely asked Jesus into your life just now, then He has come into your life as he promised. You have begun a personal relationship with God. To develop your relationship with God, it will help greatly if you find yourself a good Bible-teaching church to attend. Being in the company of like-minded people is nurturing and very helpful to your growth. You will also need a Bible (I recommend a simple translation such as the Good News Bible for starters) and that you start reading from the New Testament, beginning with the Book of Matthew.

Bringing Spiritual Life to Life in the Theatre of Life

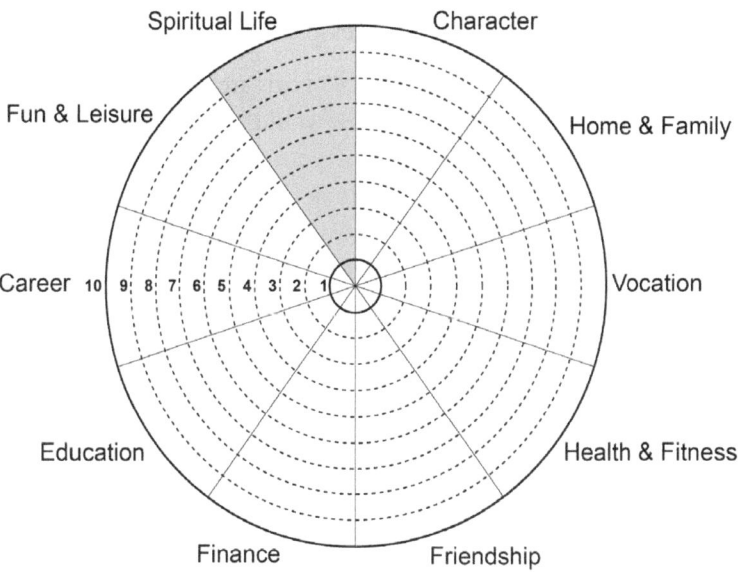

Know Thyself

The first place to begin on a journey to a fulfilled spiritual life is to identify where you currently are in the area of your spiritual life. Rate your satisfaction level by placing a mark on the wheel. Point 10 represents very satisfied and Point 0 represents very dissatisfied.

Next, identify the barriers stopping you from developing a deeper relationship with God. Is it your studies/work, or other relationships taking priority? Is it other distractions such as TV, social media, parties, etc.? Do you prefer to read the paper or engage in a great conversation with friends rather than reading the Bible or watching or listening to a Christian teaching? Or is it that you simply don't believe there is a God?

Make the Commitment

Depending on the score you gave yourself, begin to think about increasing your score to develop a stronger spiritual life by:

1. Recognising the importance of this area and the difference it will make in your life. How would you like to see yourself behaving once this area of your life has been satisfied? What would your life look like? What would your relationships look like? How would this impact your world professionally and socially?

2. You can choose to research, learn or read more about it. I recommend a book called The Purpose Driven Life by Rick Warren. This book shows us that we were created on purpose for God's purposes. You cannot truly engage with God if you do not have a meaningful relationship with Him.

Finally, bring that area into the Theatre of Life by:

1. Defining your desire for this area of your life.

2. Writing it down in detail, in positive language as though it has already happened.

3. Meditating (visualising) on what you have written.

4. Speaking out what you have written with confidence, as though it has already happened.

5. Thanking God for providing your heart's desire.

6. Go to work: apply what you have learnt from this book and from other resources – practise, practise, practise!

Chapter 13

THIS IS YOUR LIFE

> *"Now to Him who is able to [carry out His purpose and] do superabundantly more than all that we dare ask or think [infinitely beyond our greatest prayers, hopes, or dreams], according to His power that is at work within us, to Him be the glory in the church and in Christ Jesus throughout all generations forever and ever. Amen"* Ephesians 3:20-21 (AMP)

We only have **one life** here on earth, and only one opportunity to perform on the real live stage of life. Let us make every effort to make our actions count and to live a significant life here on earth. Let us take control of our lives by *'Taming Your Boss'* so that we can cultivate the discipline required to achieve a successful live.

As human beings we tend to live unbalanced lives, which can focus on the pursuit of financial wealth (amongst other things). In this pursuit, we can sometimes suffer ill-health as a result. The irony is that, even when we achieve our goals, we are still not fulfilled.

Many research studies have shown that financial wealth alone does not bring us happiness and fulfilment. I encourage you to listen to a TED talk by Robert Waldinger, the Director of the Harvard Study of Adult Development, one of the most comprehensive longitudinal studies in history. His talk is focused on a seventy-five-year study on what keeps us happy and healthy as we go through life. Suffice to say that it is the quality of our relationships with family, friends, colleagues and community that brings us happiness and fulfilment.

Financial wealth is important, yet so are our relationships, health, career, etc. We can achieve a balanced life if we choose to, and this book can help you do that by treating your life like a long-term project.

> *"...may your whole spirit and soul and body be kept blameless until our Lord Jesus Christ comes again."*
> 1 Thessalonians 5:23 (NLT)

So make the commitment and begin your journey by saying: Yes, I can! I will take control of my life by 'Taming My Boss' so that I can cultivate the discipline to put into practice the principles in this book.

> *"I can do all things through Christ who strengthens me."*
> Philippians 4:13 (NKJV)

If you haven't already, start the journey of your 'Life Project' using this book as a resource. Where are you right now on your life journey? Gauge where you are in your life right now by getting an overall snapshot using the Wholelife-10 Wheel of Life. Plotting your scores for every area on the chart will give you a snapshot of where you are in your life journey, such as the following example.

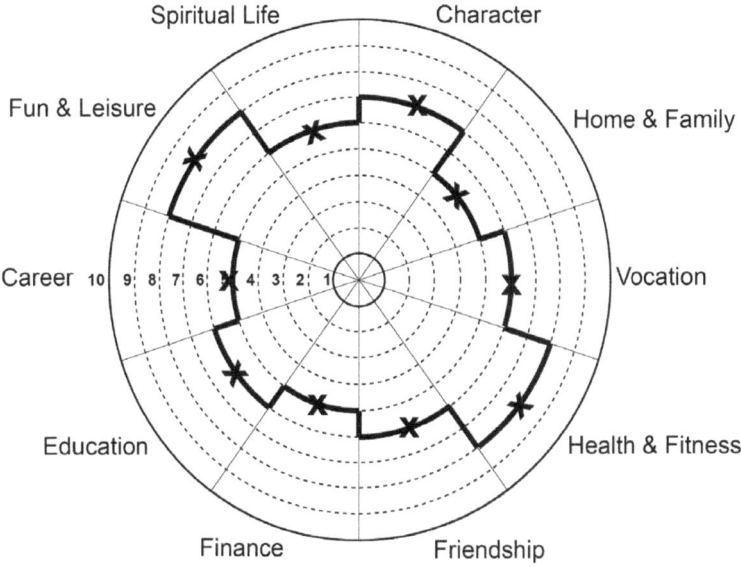

Let's begin by transferring your scores from the previous chapters onto the chart below. Rate your satisfaction level by placing an X to mark your score on the wheel. Point 10 represents very satisfied and Point 0 represents very dissatisfied.

Once you have marked a score for all ten areas, draw a continuous line through all the X points to create an overall picture such as the diagram above.

Plot your Chart as your Life is Today

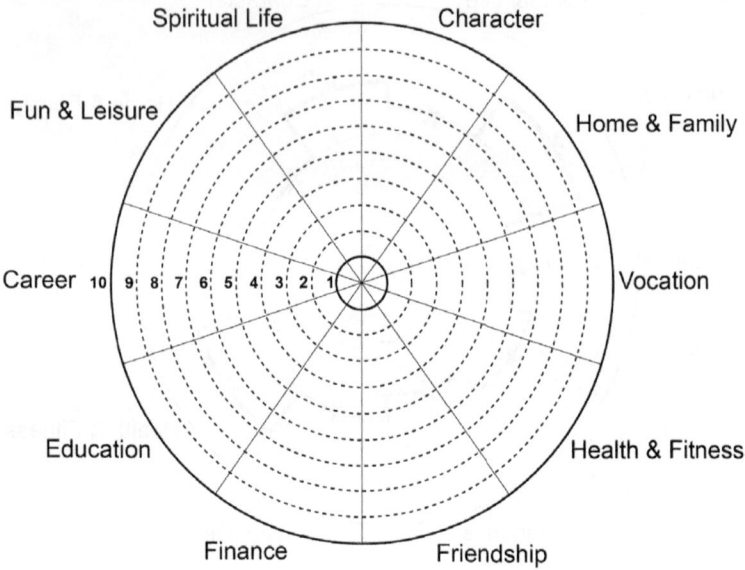

You should now have a clear picture of what your life looks like at this present time. If you are dissatisfied with the above picture, what would you like it to look like? Looking into the future, use the chart below to plot and create your desired picture for the future.

Plot your Chart for the Future

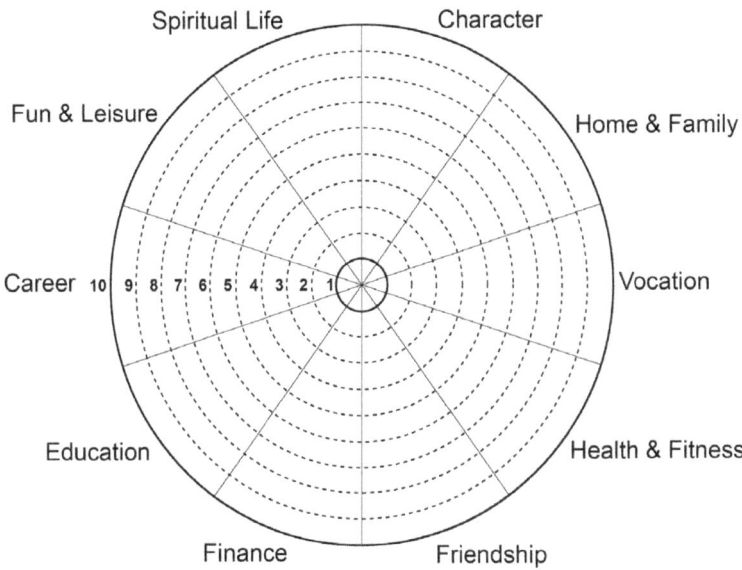

Once you have plotted your chart you can start work by bringing each area into the Theatre of Life:

1. Define your desire for this area of your life.

2. Write it down in detail, in positive language as though it has already happened.

3. Meditate (visualise) on what you have written.

4. Speak out what you have written with confidence, as though it has already happened.

5. Thank God for providing your heart's desire.

6. Go to work: apply what you have learnt from this book and from other resources – practise, practise, practise!

I hope you have enjoyed the time we have spent together as much as I have. In my short life here on earth, if I were to give a key piece of advice to my younger self, it would be this;

Life is about building strong quality relationships with God and with people; and building strong relationships with people involves shared experiences either through physical contact or by sharing information.

The benefits of the contents in this book can transform your life. As you continue to build strong quality relationships, help transform the lives of other people by sharing the wisdom in this book.

You have my best wishes for a prosperous 'Wholelife'.

*"If you can believe, **all things are possible** to him who believes."* Mark 9:23 (NKJV)